# It Sounds Fishy to Me

CARL STONES, M.D.

America Star Books
*Frederick, Maryland*

First printing

America Star Books has allowed this work to remain exactly as the author intended, verbatim, without editorial input.

Softcover 9781682291146
PUBLISHED BY AMERICA STAR BOOKS, LLLP
www.americastarbooks.pub
Frederick, Maryland

# PREFACE

Many years ago, when my mother became too deaf to converse on the telephone, I started writing her a letter every Sunday. When my kids left home, I wanted to write to them also, but then it involved writing much of the same stuff several times. When E-mail came along, it was a Godsend. I could now write my letter once and send it to all recipients. Some people thought my letters were funny and, eventually, my E-mail list grew to include several relatives and friends. Though I write about many things, I included a lot of my fishing adventures. One of my daughters, who does not like to fish, said she skips the fishing parts. Others enjoyed them, and one friend encouraged me to save some of them and put them in a binder. I never got around to the binder, but I did save a few. The rest I dredged up from memory. I had concerns that some people might read the book and think, "Man, he really thinks he is a hot fly fisherman." I am not—never will be. I have simply had the good fortune to fish with friends who are excellent fishermen and to fish some really good water. Besides, it is much more fun to write about the times I caught lots of fish than it is to write about the times I got skunked. I am dedicating this book to my wife, my children and grandchildren, but I hope that all who read it will find it entertaining. The stories are, for the most part, true. Certain conversations and situations are fictionalized, and I do admit to a little exaggeration here and there. All events are recorded as I remembered them, and it is entirely possible that my fishing buddy's recollections may be somewhat different. There are undoubtedly grammatical and punctuation errors as well as informational and factual errors. I admit to full responsibility for all of them.

# IT SOUNDS FISHY TO ME

When I die will I get my wish
To float crystal water and continue to fish
Or, into payback time will I slip
dragged through eternity with a hook in my lip?

# MY FIRST FISH

I caught my first fish using a stick with a piece of fish line attached to the end. My brother, Ben, baited my hook with a night crawler we had caught the night before crawling around on our hands and knees with a flashlight in the city park. I stood on the edge of the bridge over the Marsh Creek and dropped my worm into the water which was flowing between the streamers of moss that swayed in the current.

As soon as my bait hit the water a swarm of chubs darted out from their hiding places and began to nibble at the worm. I could feel their bumps and tugs. Finally one chub attempted too big of a bite and got itself hooked. The intermittent bumps turned to frantic thrashing. I jerked upward on my stick and threw that unfortunate chub clear over my head. Ben cackled with delight. "You just caught your first fish you lucky little snot," he hooted as he took the fish off the hook and tossed it into his fishing bag—an old WWI gas mask bag that had been purchased at an army surplus store. It turned out to be a lucky day for both of us. We caught several more chubs and then began our four mile trek home.

I was born in the small farming community called Cambridge about three miles north of Downey, Idaho. Downey sits toward the southern end of a long, narrow valley called Marsh Valley. Marsh Valley is aptly named as there is a narrow strip or marsh land that extends almost the entire length of the valley floor. The valley itself is narrow—less than 15 miles across at its widest point. A row of mountains borders it on both the east and west and at the south end Oxford Peak stands like a sentinel guarding the whole valley.

In the mountains there are numerous canyons, and small, spring fed creeks flow from most of them. The creeks from two adjacent canyons in the mountains to the east combine to form a larger stream which runs through a culvert under old route 91 near a landmark called Red Rock and thereafter meanders through the marsh some 57 miles until it empties into the Portneuf River.[1]

OXFORD PEAK

The stream is named Marsh Creek, and the two feeder creeks are, respectively, the right hand and the left hand of Marsh Creek. The two feeder creeks are crystal clear water inhabited by brook trout. Down in the marsh the water becomes colored with silt and the brookies never venture there but it is home to chubs, a few suckers and an occasional German brown trout. For reasons unknown to me, the local folks have always called Marsh Creek "The Slough." The valley is beautiful especially in the spring when everything is green. Verdant fields of winter wheat extend up the hillsides as far as the farmers can safely climb with a tractor. Some go a bit beyond safety and during my growing up years at least two farmers were killed when their tractors tipped and rolled over them.

In 1942, when I was five years old, Dad decided he had enjoyed just about all the farming he could stand, and we moved to Downey. Dad and my brothers built a house just east of the city limits. It was almost four miles from our new home to the slough bridge where I caught my first fish. Dad opened a shoe repair shop in Downey where he eked out a meager living until 1950 when he went to work for the Union Pacific Railroad, and the prosperity of the family improved markedly.

Dad was a good, kind, loving man considerate of both man and beast. He and mom both worked unimaginably hard on the farm through the years of the Great Depression and beyond. He loved flowers so our front yard was beautiful—or at least more beautiful than it would have been otherwise. He loved animals and had a special connection with them as the following story illustrates.

# QUILLED

The sun was just rising over the eastern mountains as dad stepped out of the house. A Lifetime of milking cows had conditioned him to awaken at or before dawn and moving closer to town had not changed old habits. He yawned and stretched and stood for just a moment marveling at the morning sun reflecting off Oxford Peak. It was early June, and there were still snow patches on the northern face. The June mornings were chilly, so dad buttoned his jacket and tugged at the tattered felt hat he always wore. He picked up a hoe from beside the door stoop and stepped across the yard to one of his flower gardens. He paused to admire the blooms of the early flowers and then frowned as he wondered how so many weeds and so much grass had intruded since he last was there. He sighed and began to wield the hoe against the stubborn sod.

He had worked only moments when he became aware that he was being watched. He turned to see a large brown dog sitting on the lawn about fifty feet away. "Well, old fellow," Dad asked, "where did you come from?" At the sound of his voice, the dog crouched and approached with head down and tail between his legs. As dad reached down and scratched his ears the dog brightened visibly and his tail thumped the ground appreciatively. He whined and turned away, running a few steps in the direction from which he had come. He paused and whined again. He again approached using the same submissive attitude he had shown initially. He took Dad's foot into his mouth and gave it a gentle tug before turning and running away a second time. Dad set down his hoe and followed. The dog waited until dad caught up to him and then again ran a short distance. He lead Dad out of the yard and down the street about a hundred feet. There, in the borrow pit, in an attitude of abject misery sat another stray, ears flattened and head hanging. As Dad approached, the tail of the big yellow stray began to make small, hopeful sweeps across the dust and gravel. Dad talked soothingly to the dog and reached down to scratch his ears. He was shocked to see that the dogs muzzle was virtually bristling with porcupine quills. "You poor guy," Dad said, "it sure looks like you put your nose where it didn't belong." He pondered what he should do as he stroked the dog's matted coat. Pulling quills is a painful process, and causing pain to a large unknown dog, no matter how well intended, is not something to be considered lightly. Feeling that he had to so something, however, he spoke to the dogs and started back toward the house. The dogs followed eagerly and sat on the lawn while Dad went into the house for a pair of pliers. When he returned, with some trepidation, he straddled the big dog and lifted his face, carefully placing his fingers between the quills. When he jerked the first quill the dog let out a yelp and whimpered with pain but he did not move. One by one dad jerked the quills while the dog whimpered in agony. Never once did he pull away or attempt to bite.

When the last quill was removed, dad stepped aside, and the big dog's misery instantly turned into an attitude of joy. The two dogs danced in front of Dad as though expressing their appreciation, and then they gleefully ran from the yard and disappeared down the street. Dad had never seen either dog before, and he never saw them again, but he marveled for years at the intelligence and resourcefulness of the brown dog in getting help for his buddy. Perhaps animals communicate better than we think.

# THE EVOLUTION OF A FISHERMAN

There are not many who would stretch the truth sufficiently to call the town of Downey beautiful. Most of the homes are old, and the few new ones built in recent years are mostly pre-fabs. Still, the townsfolk keep their homes and yards nice, and the town has a certain, distinct charm, and while one may not think of the word "beautiful" when viewing the town, it certainly comes to mind when viewing the valley from the town.

I feel fortunate to have grown up in Downey, and I marvel at the degree of freedom I had as a child. In this day and age it is a rare child that, at age ten, would be allowed to roam miles from home, but that is what I did. That is not to say I roamed at will. Until the day I graduated from high school Mom always knew where I was going and when I would be home. I was sixteen before I dared try, "Mom, I'm going---------" on her. I half way expected her to reply, "That's what you think, mister." To my relief she answered, "O.K. When will you be home?" In any case, as long as she knew where I was, she had no issues if I walked three or four miles to fish the Slough. When I got older, I rode my decrepit old bike but, from age eight, I thought nothing of walking long distances.

A short while after I caught my first fish our family made a trip into one of the local canyons to pick choke cherries. Ben found a birch tree growing near the creek and, from it, trimmed out a long slender limb that became my fishing pole replacing the stick I used previously. I had no reel so I wound fish line around the end of the pole, and I could lengthen it or shorten it by twisting the pole in my hands. Travelers in passing cars used to smile as they passed me trudging or riding my bicycle along Highway 91 headed for the slough where it ran below Jess Evans' place. I wore an old straw hat and worn jeans, and I carried that pole and a can of worms. I've often wondered what Norman Rockwell could have done with that scene. The only thing lacking was the fact that I was not barefoot.

When I was ten years old, Ben joined the United States Air Force. From a fishing perspective the only good thing about Ben leaving was that I inherited his telescoping fishing rod. I could no longer wind fishing line around the end of that pole, so I bought an automatic reel. In my ignorance I did not realize that this type of reel was designed for fly fishermen who fished very small streams and caught very small fish. It was like fishing with a self winding measuring tape except it was wound with fish line instead of steel tape. One could not pull much line off the spool before the spring was wound tight. Never-the-less, it worked fine for catching chubs from the slough or small brook trout from the Left Hand of Marsh Creek, my usual fishing haunts. I caught a lot of those fish, and I dutifully carried them all home. The brook trout were wonderful to eat, but the chubs required some manipulation. I gutted them, scaled them and tossed them into a pan of salt water to soak overnight. Mom said the brine leeched out the mossy taste. Mom disliked the taste of fish and would not eat them, but if I caught them she would cook them for me, usually while muttering, "ewww these stinking fish!" When she cooked them, I ate them and, as I recall, the chubs were not all that bad. The main knock to eating chubs was the fact that they are extremely bony. It is difficult to imagine that any critter could have so many ribs. Mom always made me eat home baked bread with fish as she supposed the bread would somehow keep an inadvertently swallowed bone from perforating my gut.

# THE AMPUTEES DOG

A couple of miles west of Downey, on the slough road there lived a man named Chuck Daniels (name changed) and his wife. They lived in a small cabin. Chuck was an amputee who got around on crutches. He made a meager living milking a few cows, but his "farm" otherwise was nothing but sagebrush flats. Eventually, Chuck's wife tired of the drab existence and took to running around a bit. She returned home after one of her meanderings to find that Chuck had swallowed the business end of a 12 gauge shotgun. She stuck around just long enough to dispose of his remains and to make whatever arrangements she could for the disposal of the farm, and then she left—forever as far as I know.

Left behind was Chuck's faithful dog, a large mutt that was more sheep dog than anything else. He was sort of an off-gray color with dark spots. He had a long, shaggy coat that was a matted mess and within which were embedded hundreds of cockle burrs. His long hair covered his eyes, but when that hair was parted or lifted there came into view two large, intelligent, dark brown, loving eyes. He sat for months on the step at Chuck's cabin.

Uncle Ernest Byington kept and milked cows at Chuck's place after his death. I don't know whether they belonged to him, or whether they were ones that Chuck's widow left behind. In any case, he and my cousin, Farrell, went out to Chuck's place twice a day to do the chores. I went with them one evening and met the dog. I asked Farrell who was feeding him, and he told me the dog was living on jackrabbits and mice. He was a great cow dog, and they used him to work the cows, but they never fed him anything except an occasional pan of warm milk.

One day, months after Chuck's death, a friend and I went fishing on the slough. As we passed Chuck's place on the long walk home the dog came out and greeted me like a long lost buddy. I tried to send him back, but he made it clear that he was going to be mine to do with as I saw fit. He looked normal to visual inspection, but when I petted him I was shocked. Underneath that long hair he was nothing but skin and bones. I could feel every rib, and his shoulders and hipbones were devoid of flesh. He was a walking skeleton. Even at age ten I knew this dog was in desperate straits. I knew that mom would never allow me to keep him, but I did not have the heart to turn him away.

When I arrived home and told mom my story, her first words, as expected were, "You're not keeping him." I persuaded her to feel his ribs. She, too, was shocked, and soon that pooch was wolfing down the best meal he'd apparently seen in a very long time. Mom, however, had a plan. A day or two later, Uncle Jay Evans stopped by, and Mom asked him to take the dog out to his farm. A short time later Uncle Jay's old red pickup was headed down the road with the dog in the back, and my hope that Mom would change her mind and let me keep him dissipated.

Uncle Jay already had two dogs, and he did not need a third, so he gave the dog to Len Hickman, his son-in-law's father. By remarkable coincidence, Len was an amputee who got around on crutches—just like Chuck Daniels. It was a match made in heaven. Len declared later that it was the best dog he ever had. The dog learned to open the gate to Len's pasture. In the morning, Len would get out of bed, go to his bedroom window and whistle. The dog would run out to the pasture, open the gate, round up the cows and bring them to the barn. Len had only to go to the barn and do the milking. When the chores were done, the dog took the cows back to the pasture and sat blocking the gate until Len could get there to close it. I suppose the dog would have happily milked the cows also had he been physically able. The dog seemed to have a well developed awareness of Len's handicap and was always there to assist him. An inseparable bond developed between the two.

I had occasion to go to Len's place with my cousin, Jimmy Evans, one time and the dog joyfully greeted me as if he remembered my kindness. Now one could not feel his ribs. He was sleek, happy and obviously well cared for. I have often thought what a terrible shame it would have been had such a remarkable animal died from starvation.

# THE LONG WALK

Duane Heidenreich and I walked to the slough to fish. It was the route we had walked previously past Chuck Daniels' place but, for some reason, we did a whole lot more walking that day than usual, and by the time I walked the four miles home my ten year old legs ached miserably. Dad had degenerative arthritis and, from time to time, his knuckles or toes would become painful, and when they did he painted them with HEET linament. I thought that if HEET worked for his knuckles, it ought to work for my aching legs, so I went into the bathroom and applied that linament from my crotch to my feet. For a few moments, everything was fine, and then my legs turned bright red, and I was on fire. I suddenly realized why the linament got its name. I tried to eat supper, but the longer I sat the more intense the burning became. I paced the floor and wept. I filled the bathtub with water and tried to wash the linament off, but that just made the burning worse. I spent a sleepless, miserable night but, thankfully, the effect of the linament finally wore off, and I've had nothing to do with HEET since. There was one thing about it, though, with my skin on fire I never gave another thought to my aching muscles. Does that constitute a cure?

# TANTALIZING TROUT

My dad did not fish so after Ben left home I had no one to teach me. Most of the fishing I did as a youth I learned on my own or from my fishing companions who, for the most part, didn't know much more than I did.

One day Claire Evans and I were fishing the Slough, and we wandered over to Pete Jensen's pond. It was a small body of crystal clear water fed by a large spring, and it drained into Marsh Creek just a few feet away. Claire and I were standing watching huge carp stirring up mud. I peered into the spring. "Holy cow," I shouted, "Claire come look at this." Claire moved beside me and looked over the edge. There, almost motionless, lurking down in the depths was a huge rainbow trout. We dropped to our knees thinking it would keep the fish from seeing us. With great excitement we dropped our worm baited hooks down into the spring and jigged them in front of the fish's snout. The fish paid no attention. The only time it moved was when one of our worms touched it and even then it was just a matter of moving slightly aside. We changed our bait to salmon eggs, but the fish's reaction was exactly the same—complete disinterest. We tried chumming the hole by dropping single eggs into the spring, but they simply dropped untouched down the bottomless hole. Now completely frustrated, we changed to spinners which we jigged up and down front of its face, but nothing enticed that fish. We probably wasted an hour trying to catch it but finally gave up. We considered trying to spear it, but it was too deep in the hole and we had nothing to spear it with. Man, we hated getting beat by that fish.

Discouraged, we switched back to our worms and, with no expectation whatsoever, Claire gave his hook a half-hearted toss across the pond. It started to settle toward the bottom, and suddenly his line took off. There was a large whoosh and splash, and a large carp bent his pole double. It must have been about 30 inches. It raced around the pond stirring mud as it went and then headed for the outlet, and there was nothing Claire could do to stop it. We were laughing deliriously. Suddenly, his line went limp, and the fish was gone, along with his hook and a good portion of his leader. Claire stood for a moment with a bemused look, and then we both began to laugh. Trash fish or no trash fish that carp was the biggest fish Claire had ever hooked, and it was the biggest fish I had ever seen hooked. Our interest in fishing was suddenly rekindled. It took considerable time for our adrenalin to return to normal, and we spent the remainder of the afternoon lamenting the huge fish that got away and trying, without success, to catch another. The trout, meanwhile, remained unfazed in his hole at the bottom of the spring.

# THE BOY SCOUTS

At age twelve I joined the boy scouts which were a source of great fun and adventure, especially in the summer. The best thing about our troop was the summer encampment when our leaders took us on a five or six day trek to an alpine lake, usually in the Idaho Primitive Area. My very first trip was to the Palisades Lake near the Wyoming border. That was before the Palisades Dam was built. The lake was rather small back then and it wasn't an alpine lake, but a substantial hike was required to get there, or so it seemed at the time. It was on that trip that I met Claire Evans. He was thereafter my best friend until I graduated from high school. He and I, being the youngest and the smallest boys in the troop, arrived at the lake dead last, dead tired and just in time to fix dinner. I don't know what Claire ate but I cooked up a box of Lipton's navy bean soup. Back then this dehydrated soup came in a little square box, and it really didn't weigh much. It really was quite good, and it was easy to fix so it was a popular item for back packing—at least for me. You just had to add water and heat it up. Tired as we were, it was barely fully dark when we crawled, fully clothed, into our sleeping bags. My ears got cold but after eating all those beans sleeping with my head in the bag was not a desireable option. It rained that night and, since we were sleeping in the open, my borrowed sleeping bag got wet. I hung it up during the day but it did not completely dry, and I shivered in that wet bag the rest of the trip. I'm not sure I got it thoroughly dry before I returned it to the owner, and he must have been thrilled about loaning it to me.

On our summer camp outs we were always accompanied by a scout master and, usually, two additional adult men and one or two pack horses. One of the horses carried a large, rolled up rubber raft and a small gas outboard motor. The adults spent most of their day in the boat trolling while we youngsters tried to fish off the bank. We always got a turn in the boat, and it usually consisted of one trip across the lake and back. I had no trolling gear so I used a spare pole belonging to one of the adults. I had the privilege of dragging an orange flat fish through the water, and I didn't get so much as a nibble. It was not lost on me that all of the adults were using long trolling gears (Pop Gears or Cow Bells) with a baited hook on the end. THEY were catching fish! It also was not lost on me that only the boys took turns in the boat. The adults acted as if they were glued to the seats.

Once back on shore I tried to cast, but that automatic reel was worthless. I couldn't get my bait more than ten feet out into the water. I caught no fish on that trip, but Claire Evans, Thayne Vaughan and I discovered a raft somebody before us had made by lashing pieces of drift wood together. We had no paddles, so we fashioned some poles which we used to push us around in shallow water. When we shoved off into deeper water we tried to use the poles as paddles. Tom Sawyer and Huck Finn had nothing over on us. We managed to move a little bit as, fortunately, there was no wind. We played on that raft for hours and then poled our way toward shore. The little bay was jammed with floating logs, so we got as close to the shore as we could and hopped from log to log the rest of the way. We had barely set foot on shore when we heard a gurgling sound. We turned back and stood agog as the waterlogged raft slowly sank. "Geeeez," Claire exclaimed, and he began to laugh. Thayne and I favored each other with a nervous glance and then joined in. Why had the raft not sunk in deep water with us on it? The Lord loves foolish boys, I guess.

With no raft to play on we spent the rest of the trip hiking around, playing in the icy water, eating half cooked food and getting filthy dirty. The best part of the camp-out was the second night when I awakened to shouting and a wild commontion and saw the scout master standing like an apparition in his white, long drawers, barn door flapping, pounding a porcupine over the head with a boat oar. He had awakened when old porky stuck his wet nose into his ear.

I considered that first camp out to be a learning experience, and when I returned home, as soon as I was able, I bought a decent reel and a long, silver Pop Gear. I bought a couple of bottles of fingernail polish and painted red and green stripes across the convex surfaces of the Pop Gear spoons. I was sure that on the next trip I would certainly catch fish. I had no chance to test it but, inevitably, the next summer rolled around and we made the long hike into an alpine lake. I cannot remember which one. What I do remember, though, is that when I prepared for my turn in the boat I discovered that the only leader I had was some catgut rolled on a stick that I had dug out of Dad's old tackle box. It was probably almost as old as he was. It was rather brittle but I tested it while dry, and it seemed strong. What I didn't realize was that once it got thoroughly soaked it had the tensile strength of a strand of spaghetti. I afixed a length of that leader onto the end of my line and tied on a snap swivel to which I attached my pop gear. I added a snelled hook to the end, baited it with a piece of night crawler and waited for my turn in the boat. Finally, I climbed aboard and the boat started across the lake. I eagerly paid out my line and waited, confident of success. Suddenly my pole bent from a smashing hit. "I've got a fish" I screamed—and then the line went slack. A very large trout erupted from the water with my Pop Gear dangling from his jaw, and that was the last I ever saw of it.

One of our summer campouts involved a long drive over an unimproved dirt road to reach the trail head. It was hardly a road at all, and it had dangerously sharp curves around hills and through trees. In two places it crossed boggy meadows where the trucks sank to their axles. The pack horses were unloaded from their trailer and used to tow the trucks through the muck while we boy scouts pushed. The spinning wheels from the truck covered some of us from head to toe with gooey mud much to the delight of those who avoided the splatter. It was common for us to get dirty during the course of a camp week, but on this trip we got a flying start. To keep weight off the trucks we all did a lot more hiking than had been intended, but our spirits were light, and once across the bog we were able to ride once again. Once at the trailhead our hiking began in earnest. We immediately set out up a steep mountainside which involved numerous switchbacks. Near the summit there was a large ridge, and just over the ridge lay a large lake—our destination. The trail continued past this lake up a steep incline for another half mile or so to another small lake. For some reason, Claire Evans, Thayne Vaughan, Beauford Morgan (name changed) and I decided to camp about half way between the two lakes. It was a terrible place for a camp. The rocky ground sloped, there was no shade and it was completely dry. We had to hike to one or the other of the lakes to get water to cook or clean up. It had only one advantage. It was completely out of sight and ear shot of the scout master or any of the adults.

The day after we made camp we decided to hike to the upper lake to fish. It was said to be stocked with California golden trout, a species we had never seen, and we were eager to catch a few. On the way to the lake we encountered two young adult men who had hiked into the lakes expecting to find solitude and instead were disgusted to find the place overrun with boy scouts. They were not at all happy to see us and showed little in the way of restraint concerning their unhappiness. One of the men made a snide comment regarding the four of us. We were, in his view, a bunch of little shits as I recall. He wasn't all that offensive, but it was enough to set Beauford off. I cannot, nor would I want to, remember all the colorful insults he hurled back. The one exchange I do remember was Beauford screaming, "Your ears are so floppy you could piss in them" and one of the guys retorting, "You don't seem much like boy scouts to me." The guys had about decided they were going to kick some boy scout hiney, but we got Beauford shut up and disappeared up the mountainside.

On the morning we were to break camp Claire, Thayne, Beauford and I slept in a bit, ate a leisurely breakfast, took our time packing our sleeping bags, tent and other gear and then sauntered down the trail toward the main camp. When we crested a small ridge we discovered, to our shock and dismay, that there was no camp. We looked beyond the lake down the mountain, and there, a mile below us in the valley, was a convoy of trucks already winding their way toward the meadows. We were being left! Our leisure attitude changed to complete panic. We left the trail with all of its switch-backs and started a head long plunge down the mountain, trying to obtain an angle that would intercept the trucks. We had gone only a short distance when Beauford, who was obese, began complaining that he could go no farther. Claire, Thayne and I told Beauford to make his way down as fast as he could and Claire and I took his pack and continued charging down the hill, holding the pack between us while Thayne ran ahead to try to head off the trucks. We broke out of the timber onto the meadow just as the trucks were passing about fifty yards away. We yelled as loud as we could, and finally one of the scouts in the back of a pick-up saw us. The adults were mortified that they had left without us, but they covered their embarassment by chewing us out for camping away from the main group. Beauford finally came straggling out of the timber, and we continued without incident. We never even got stuck in the mud on the way down. Thereafter the scout leaders always made us camp close together. As for the fishing—it really wasn't much. We caught enough California goldens to know what they looked like and not much more.

# SALVESON'S DOG

When I was fifteen, Texie Thomas hired me to mow her lawn and do yard work. Just down the hill from her place was a family named Salveson, and they had a large, brown dog. It did not matter whether I passed their place on foot or on my bicycle that dog came after me. He never did bite but if I was on foot he would approach me until he was close enough to bite, all the while barking and growling and generally daring me to take another step. He intimidated the crap out of me. If I rode my bicycle it was worse. He would come roaring out of the yard and grab at my pant legs. I usually had to get off my bike and wheel it past their place on foot, with the bike between me and the dog. Man, I hated that animal. One day when I was sixteen I had occasion to rummage around the old shed behind our house. I ran across the old birch fishing pole Ben had trimmed for me many years previously. Inspiration struck. Just weeks earlier I had purchased an old '35 Chevy Coupe (my first car) so I climbed aboard, rolled down the window and held that old birch pole over the top of the car. Driving with one hand, I turned past Texie's place and headed down the hill. As I approached Salveson's home that dog came roaring out as I knew he would and began nipping at my left front tire. I whipped that birch pole down as hard as I could and caught the dog squarely across the back. He let out a surprised yelp and ran for his yard while giving me disbelieving looks over his shoulder. The next day I deliberately rode my bike past the Salvesons. The old dog just sat on the back steps and watched me go by. He never bothered me again.

By the time I graduated from high school I had a pretty good idea how to fish small streams, how to recognize structure where fish were likely to be holed up and how to troll in lakes. I had acquired a pair of hip waders and a creel. The fish I then caught during the summer baked in a wicker basket instead of Ben's old gas mask bag. Some of the fish I caught on hot, summer days were in pretty sorry shape by the time I got them home, but I ate them anyway. I did most of my fishing in either the right hand or the left hand of Marsh Creek, and my favorite technique was to wade into the stream and let my bait float down the stream into a hole. I actually caught a lot of fish. My biggest mistake at that point in my life was that I thought I actually knew something about fishing. It was not until years later that I discovered that I really didn't know beans about anything

# EVERYTHING IN ITS SEASON

Ecclesiastes 3:1 "To everything there is a season and a time for every purpose under the heaven." When I was a youth, fishing season in our part of Idaho opened the middle of April and closed around the end of October. My friends and I used to eagerly look forward to opening day, and we went fishing almost without fail. The only problem was, every fisherman in the valley was out fishing somewhere on that day, and the worst thing that could happen was to go to one of our favorite spots and find out my cousin's husband, Earl Merideth had fished the holes just ahead of us. Earl was one of the few fly fishermen I knew, and he was good at it. If he was ahead of us, we may just as well pack it in and go home. Fishing limits on Brookies were generous in those days, and I can still, in my mind, hear Earl cackling as he showed us his creel full of fish while we stood gaping with nothing to show for our efforts.

When I graduated from high school, I entered into a long season of non-fishing. It was the season for getting an education and settling into a career. With one exception, I did not fish for 10 years. I moved to Salt Lake City and went to work at the old Cudahy Meat Packing Company where I toiled in the ham department. It was a pretty good job at the time, but the main thing I learned, aside from some really ribald jokes, was that I did not want to spend my life pushing hams around overhead racks. It was during this time that I had my one fishing experience. A guy I shall call Phil, because I can no longer remember his real name, worked with me at the ham table. We started talking about fishing one day, and he said he drove to Kemmerer, Wyoming from time to time, and there was a river along the road that he was dying to drop a hook into. A young guy named Lamar Noble and I were easily persuaded. One Friday evening after work we piled into Phil's car and headed for Kemmerer.

We needed Wyoming fishing licenses, so after we crossed the Wyoming border we stopped at our earliest opportunity. It was dark by then, but we spotted a bar that sold licenses, so Phil pulled into the parking lot. It was an old wooden building with sinage compliments of Pabst Blue Ribbon. There were a few cars pulled up next to the building, so we added ours to the line and went inside. There was juke box music playing, and several cowboys were sitting on stools at the bar. We bought our licenses and Phil and Lamar decided it would be nice to have a beer. The bar tender looked us over and asked for I.D., so Lamar, who was barely 21 produced his. The bar tended checked it carefully and handed it back. Phil then produced his, and while the bar tender was looking at it Lamar slipped his I.D. back to me. I was only 18. The bar tender did not see the maneuver, but the cowboys at the bar did, and they roared with laughter. Phil and Lamar ordered beers and Phil handed out small cigars. I did not smoke, but I was in the process of playing the man of the world, so I took one and lit up. I took one puff and nearly choked to death. I was trying my best not to cough and was failing miserably. Since I was trying to hold it back, each supressed cough caused a sharp contraction of my abdomen followed by puffing of my cheeks and staccato explosions through my lips. Now the cowboys were almost falling off their bar stools. We drank our beers, and once again we hit the road.

About midnight we pulled into a camp ground near a good sized river and pulled out our sleeping bags. Since our trip was sort of impromptu, we had not packed any food. We had thought we would get what we needed at a store along the way and eat lots of fish. Once we got into Wyoming, there were no stores. There was the river, a scattered ranch house here and there and a whole lot of jack rabbits. All we had with us was a little bit of junk food. We nibbled on that and went to bed.

At the crack of dawn we got up, finished off the junk food and waded into the river. We would catch our dinners. All of us had hip boots so we couldn't wade in water that was very deep. The river was wide, but fortunately it was shallow. I baited up with a worm and tried my Marsh Creek technique, wading down the river and letting the bait float ahead of me. We fished all day and never touched a fish. I then realized, to my chagrine, that maybe I really didn't know as much about fishing as I thought I did. Evening rolled around and, since we had caught no fish, we still had nothing to eat. We were not only discouraged but, again, we went to bed hungry.

We awoke Sunday morning, and I have never been so hungry in my life. I was famished! Down the road across from the camp ground we spotted an old farm house. It was little more than a shack with some rotting out buildings, but in the corral there were a few milk cows standing knee deep in manure. We trudged down the road, climbed the small hill to the house and knocked on the door. A skinny, elderly, unshaven old man wearing manure caked overalls opened the door and regarded us warily. Who the hell knocks on doors at the crack of dawn? We asked if we could buy food, and he sold us a couple of quarts of the most expensive milk ever stripped from a cow. The old man may not have been prosperous, but he knew suckers when he saw them. We paid gladly, and that warm milk which probably had an E. coli count off the charts was absolutely delicious.

After a year of the kind of toil I did at Cudahy, I did not yet have enough money saved to go to college. The military draft was still in effect in those days, and one of the guys at the packing plant advised me to get the military out of the way while I was still single, so I volunteered for the draft and entered the United States Army. After a two year hitch in the army, there followed three years of college and four years of medical school. I had not much liked my years in the service as a grunt, so I thought the last thing I would ever consider would be going back into the army, but after years of enjoying student povery at its finest I found that the army had a very appealing program for medical students. I re-entered the service on the army's Senior Program which paid me as a First Lieutenant my senior year. I then owed them two years of payback time but, since I had to be in the army anyway, it was appealing to continue my training while receiving army pay. Civilian internship and residency programs considered your training to be your pay, so for those years you generally received only room and board and a very small stipend. I was accepted at the Tripler Army Medical Center in Hawaii for a rotating internship and was promoted to a Captain. My older brother, who was already a physician, said regarding my internship: "If you are going to get your ass worked off it may as well be in exotic surroundings." The army was good to me, and I eventually retired after 20 yrs. of service as a full Colonel.

# FISHING WASHINGTON

When I finished my internship, I moved to Tacoma Washington to begin my residency in pathology at the Madigan Army Medical Center. Western Washington is spectacularly beautiful, and Tacoma sits right on the edge of Puget Sound. The climate is cool, frequently overcast and notorious for the almost constant mist-like rain. Cloudless days do occur, however, and when they do Mt. Rainier looks as if it were almost suspended in the eastern sky. The awe inspiring beauty of a single clear day makes up for numerous overcast ones. Rivers and lakes are numerous, and it did not take long for me to once again crave the thrill of doing battle with a fish.

In the spring of 1967 I found a small apartment on the shore of American Lake. Karl Luken and his wife owned a large home which was built on a hillside above the lake, and their beautiful lawn extended almost to the water's edge. There was a nice dock extending into the water. The Lukens lived in the upper level of the house and rented out the lower level which opened onto that beautiful lawn. It was a perfect bachelor pad—living room, kitchen and single bedroom. The bathroom was so small I almost had to back into it to sit on the commode, but it also had a small shower, sink and a mirror. What more did I need? Karl allowed me to park my car in a garage at the top of the hill and, later, when I bought a boat I was permitted to tie it up at the dock. I was very much into water skiing at the time, but American Lake was good fishing for kokanee and rainbow trout, and I caught my share. The Lukens dock was right next to Bill's Boat House, so when I wanted to fish for kokanee I had but to walk to the water's edge, step around the fence separating the two properties, stroll into the bait shop and buy a carton of fly maggots. There were two main ways to catch Kokanee. I successfully trolled for them using a long Pop Gear at the end of which was a small ring shaped lure studded with tiny red beads called a Wedding Band. The hook was baited with a row of maggots hung by their tails. It was very effective. The other effective way to catch them was to string a fly rod with spinning line then park your boat in a well known deep hole where kokanee were known to hang out, drop your bait clear to the bottom and jig it mildly. The fly rod was desirable because the kokanee would barely mouth the bait and it took a sensitive touch to detect the bite. The kokanee grew large in American Lake with many weighing around three pounds.

Trout fishing was usually best in an extension off the lake called, "Little Lake." I usually trolled with the same Pop Gear set-up that I used for kokanee but without the Wedding Band. I used night crawlers for bait.

In addition to American Lake there was the whole Puget Sound and Pacific Coast to be fished. Out in the Sound I caught rock rod, flounder, ling cod, dogfish sharks—you name it. Ling cod may not be the ugliest fish in all creation but it was certainly the ugliest fish I ever caught.

Washington has numerous crystal clear rivers, and I wasted a few trips trying to catch trout before I learned that most of those rivers fish well for andromatous fish only. You have to be on the river when the fish are running. I had never fished for steelhead and, in fact, had never even seen one but after all the glowing reports I had heard about these marvelous fish I had to try it. I bought a steelhead rod and reel, silver lures, golden lures, lures with red corks, lures with red beads, you name it. I made a few trips to some of the nearby rivers but I had no idea where or how to fish for steelies and, of course, I caught nothing. Most importantly, I did not know that you had to wait for a run or there were no fish in the river. I became convinced that steelhead were nothing but a myth. Then Clea and I made a trip to the Pacific Coast and camped in a park at a little settlement called Quinault. On the bulletin board next to the outhouse there was posted the name and phone number of a fishing guide. I found a pay telephone (no cell phones back then) and gave him a call. He said that there were no fish running the rivers at that time so I was out of luck. I gave him my phone number and asked him to call me when the fishing was good.

A few weeks later, I got a call. He said there was a summer run of steelhead in the Hoh river. I put in a request at the hospital for three days of leave, but by the time it was approved and I got to Quinault several days had passed. I met the guide who was a wiry little guy about 5'6" with a three day growth of beard named Frank Cush (ficticious name). He told me that particular summer steelhead run had lasted only three days and was almost over, but he thought we could catch some stragglers, so bright and early the next morning we launched his river boat into the Hoh. He baited my hook with a large gob of salmon eggs tied up in cheesecloth that he had cured himself using Borax, and we began a long drift. I was fascinated by how adept Frank was at rowing against the current and positioning the boat. That water was moving fast, and he had no chance to rest. The muscles in his arms were like steel bands, and he was tireless. He would hold the boat almost stationary in the current and nod his head toward an eddy or a log jam and say, "Cast over there." I'd make a couple of casts, catch nothing and we'd drift down to the next hole. I didn't know if there were no fish or if I was inept, but I fished all day with nothing to show for it, and my belief that steelhead were a myth was solidified. Frank was witty and entertaining so it was a fun outing in spite of no fish.

Finally, at about four o'clock, Frank nodded toward a curve in the bank where a large pile of brush was trapped, and there was a deep hole just in front of it. I made my cast and the salmon eggs sank into the hole and began swirling in the eddy. Suddenly, my line shot out of the hole and into the current, and a large steelhead rose into the air. My drag was set tight, but that fish was ripping off line and the reel was absolutely screaming. The fish leaped again, and I managed to turn it, but it took great effort to haul it upstream. Every time I thought I was making decent headway, the fish turned and took off. Soon, my arms were aching, so I braced the handle of the rod against my chest and moved my right hand farther up the pole. The increased leverage helped, but I began to wonder if I was going to outlast that fish. I had never before hooked a fish that fought for so long. It took me almost 20 minutes to bring it to the net. It was a nice 12 lb. hen that was so fresh from the ocean that it still had a few sea lice on it. It was the only fish I caught that day, but I thoroughly felt the trip was worth it. Yes, Virginia, steelhead are the real deal! Moreover, those steelhead filets were absolutely delicious.

# FISHING WITH DAD AND FONZO

In late July of 1967 my parents came to visit me, and they were accompanied by two friends, Fonzo and Lottie Dewey, whom they had known since before they were all married. Neither Mom nor Dad much enjoyed driving, but Fon did, so with him at the wheel, they made the long trip from Downey, Idaho to Tacoma, taking two days. Neither couple had been to Tacoma, and they were completely fascinated by the majestic scenery of Western Washington. I took a week of leave and did my utmost to show them what Washington had to offer. We made a trip to Mt. Ranier Park, picked wild strawberries, and toured American Lake in my boat.

Dad and Fon had never been salmon fishing, so I made arrangements to get the three of us onto a charter boat out of Westport Washington which sits on the Pacific Coast about eighty miles from Tacoma. Westport is located at the mouth of a large harbor, and charter fishing is a huge industry for the small town. One can charter for tuna, bottom fish or salmon. At that time, the limit for salmon was three fish. On a charter boat, the skipper does not care who catches the fish. Fishing continues until either the time limit expires, or the boat limits out—whichever comes first. If one individual were to catch ten fish he would be permitted to disembark with only three of them, but he could pick the three that he wanted. If the boat limited, everybody left with three fish. Every fish had to be accounted for on somebody's salmon punch card.

The night before our great fishing safari, Mom and Lottie packed a large, wonderful lunch. The charter boats leave the harbor just after dawn so Dad, Fon and I left Tacoma around 3 A.M. Almost as soon as we were underway I began to have second thoughts. I was worried that Dad and Fon (both almost seventy) would get sea sick, and I wondered what kind of misery I had set those poor old geezers up for. We arrived at Westport in time for our appointment, but we were among the last arrivals. On a charter boat there are places on the boat that are more desirable than others to fish from. The best places are around the stern, and the worst places are on the bow.

When the boat stops moving forward it rolls back and forth, and the bow lifts and drops in the swells. It is the most likely place to get sea sick. The fishing is usually better on the stern. Cut Herring is used for bait and it is dropped to the bottom and jigged. From the stern one could more or less control the jig whereas on the bow the lifting and dropping of the boat did the jigging for you. It is much easier to stand steady on the stern without all the pitching and rolling. Arriving near the last, as we did, we got the very worst place on the boat—alongside the cabin toward the bow. The deck is narrow between the cabin and the rail making it difficult to stand steady, and we were far enough forward to get the full effect of the rocking motion. Now I was really worried about Dad and Fon.

There are numerous charter boats in Westport, all preparing to depart at the same time. The skippers and their assistants fire up the motors when they first go on board, so all those diesel motors have been idling for an hour or so before the boats depart. The harbor air becomes heavy with the stink of diesel smoke, and by the time we left the pier I was half sick from inhaling the fumes. I was certain Dad and Fon could be no better off. I said nothing about how I was feeling, and I assumed they, also, were just keeping mum.

We left the harbor and started over the bar. I have never entirely understood just what the "bar" is, but it is apparently bottom structure between the harbor and the ocean which amplifies the wave action of the water. It takes several minutes to cross, and the going is invariably rough. Conventional wisdom is, if you can get over the bar without getting sea sick you have it made. I definitely did not have it made that day. Since I was half sick to begin with it did not take the the bar long to finish the job. I was staring at the horizon which is the recommended way to combat seasickness. The idea is that if you keep your eyes steady you will fool your inner ear into thinking it isn't being scrambled. My inner ear knew better.

I was soon dreadfully nauseated. I was thinking death would be a welcome relief but I feared I might have to start feeling about fifty percent better in order to die. Surely if I were feeling this bad Dad and Fon must be near death's door. We were all sitting on the deck with our backs against the outside of the cabin, and we had about an hours ride ahead of us to reach the fishing area. Suddenly Dad turned to me and said, "Say, we ought to eat that lunch Mom packed for us." I leaped to my feet and headed for the rail. My stomach turned wrong side out and those two old gomers actually began eating! They thought my misery was funny. Once I had tossed my cookies I felt considerably better, but there was nothing I could do but wistfully watch those sandwiches disappear. There was no way I was going to hold anything down.

Soon we reached the fishing area. The skipper's assistant ran our hooks through the cut Herring and we dropped our bait overboard. I instructed Dad to let his bait fall clear to the bottom (about 60 ft.), retrieve it about 6 ft. and then begin jigging it. Dad had scarcely begun jigging his herring when his line took off, and his reel started screaming. A large king salmon erupted into the air and crashed back into the water. It probably weighed about forty pounds and was really ripping line off Dad's reel. I Yelled, "Yay, Dad, way to go," and I turned toward him just in time to see him drop his thumb onto the spool of the reel. "NOOOOOO," I screamed, but it was too late. His thumb hit that spool, and his 20 pound leader snapped like a piece of cotton thread. Dad stood, his line slack, looking disappointed and a little befuddled. I felt like screaming, "MAN, THAT WAS A DUMB THING TO DO," but this was my dad, after all, so I just choked out between sobs, "Dad, you have to just set your drag and let those big fish run." It was the only king hooked that day.

The wonders of fishing truly amaze me. I had fished for salmon only a few times, and it was the first time for Dad and Fon. We boarded late, so we got the worst places on the boat, and neither of those old gents had a clue how to catch salmon yet Fon caught more than anybody else on the boat. Dad was a close second, and he hooked the only king. I caught the third most Salmon, and if we counted the sea bass we landed, I actually had the most fish. As soon as those fish started biting the seasickness somehow vanished, and we had a phenomenal day. We went to a cannery and traded all but one salmon for canned fish and headed home. We grilled and ate that fresh salmon, and it was indescribably delicious.

I had felt rather guilty leaving Mom and Lottie at my apartment while we men were out having fun, but when we got home we found the women bubbling with excitement. Unknown to me, my landlord was a pilot, and he took the two women up in a small plane and flew them all over Puget Sound. Neither of them had been in a small aircraft before and they had a marvelous time.

# ALASKA

The four years of my residency passed rapidly, but much was accomplished. On November 10, 1967 at the age of 30 I married Clea Ann Gibson.

CARL AND CLEA WEDDING

I became board eligible in both clinical and anatomical pathology, and it was time to move on. I received orders assigning me as the Chief of Pathology at the Bassett Army Hospital in Ft. Wainwright, Alaska. Clea and I bought a Toyota Landcruise and set out for Fairbanks. By the time we reached the Alcan Highway, there was a distinct chill in the air, and it rained every night. The rain made camping miserable, but the rain was a good thing since it settled the dust. Without it that unpaved highway would have been enveloped in a cloud of dust, and we'd have seen little of the truly spectacular scenery.

Toward the end of our third day we arrived at a restaurant and motel located absolutely in the middle of nowhere. The parking lot was a sea of mud which extended right up to the doorways of the motel rooms. We decided we'd had enough camping in the rain so we rented a room for the night. When we opened the door to our room we discovered that the mud did not stop at the doorway. We beheld the dirtiest, mud caked floor one could imagine. I returned to the motel office and complained that the floor needed to be cleaned, and then we sat in the Landcruiser and waited.

After a few minutes a very fat Indian woman waddled out of the motel office carrying a wet mop but no bucket of water. She waded across the mud and into the room without wiping her feet. She then proceeded to swing the mop back and forth across the floor never once rinsing it out. When the floor was completely wet she left.

When the floor dried it was as dirty as ever—maybe worse. She had done nothing but re-arrange the dirt. The beds appeared to be clean so Clea and I decided we'd just avoid walking barefoot. A little later we went to the café for dinner. It was a small place consisting of a counter separated from the kitchen by a wall with a large opening to pass the food through. We could see the cook in the back, and he was wearing the greasiest, filthiest apron I'd ever seen. We reluctantly ordered pork chops which he fried in a pan that may have sat unwashed on the stove for an eternity, but I had utter faith that it would get sterilized as the meat cooked. To our delight the pork chops and fried potaties were absolutely delicious. I think they were the best I've ever eaten. To our even greater delight we did not get sick from either the food or the stay in the motel.

As we drove, it seemed as if there were rivers and lakes everywhere, and the whole landscape was spectacular. Many times a river followed alongside the highway, and every rapids, bend and hole induced in me an almost overwhelming urge to stop and fish. I could hardly wait to finish the trip and get my affairs in order so I could try my luck. The nightly rains turned to snow a couple of days before we got to Fairbanks, and we had to drive slowly on the slickened roads, but we arrived safely on 9 September, 1970. The snow was on the ground to stay, though, so my fishing ardor was somewhat cooled. Winter came early.

# FISHING THROUGH THE ICE

I learned that there was a lake not far from Fairbanks that was said to be populated with Arctic grayling. One balmy November day (anything warmer than -10 degrees was considered balmy) I decided I simply had to get out and fish somewhere. I had never seen a grayling, and I had never in my life been ice fishing, but I rented an auger and set out to see what I could do. It was an exercise in ignorance if not total stupidity. It was -5 degrees outside, so I bundled up in woolen underwear, cargo pants, my army issued parka with a wolf ruff on the hood, my Mickey Mouse boots (the thick double layered, air filled boots the army issued—they did, indeed look like Mickey Mouse feet), and mittens and I was off.

When I arrived at the lake there was no one else there. That should have told me something. I knew nothing of the lake—where it was shallow, where it was deep—and I knew nothing of the fish or where fish were likely to hang out if, indeed, there were any fish. Never-the-less I walked out on the ice, shoveled away the snow and began drilling a hole with the auger. I twisted and turned that thing until I thought my arms would fall off. For a few bucks more I could have rented a gas powered one, but no, I thought this was going to be easy. On the positive side, it was the only time on the whole trip when I was warm. The ice was deep and the going was tough, but I was persistent and finally I broke though. I then took a number six hook, baited it with a big wad of nightcrawler and dropped it through the hole. Since there was no way to accomplish this with mittens on I pulled them off and my fingers quickly became stiff. I had no idea whether I should fish deep or shallow, but at least I had my bait in the water.

I jigged the bait up and down until my feet got cold, and I got tired of doing it, so then I propped my pole on the edge of the hole. How can one's feet get cold buried in two inch thick, air inflated boots that are like walking around on pillows? It was miserably cold, and there was a moderate breeze blowing, adding to the chill factor. I walked around, stomped my feet, flailed my arms, ran in place and put my hands under my armpits. No matter what I did I could not keep warm. I had seen pictures of ice fishermen in Minnesota and Wisconsin sitting in little huts drinking coffee (or something stronger), and I came to realize that there was more to enjoying ice fishing than drilling a hole in the ice. I had no hut, no heater, nothing hot to drink, and I caught exactly nothing. I concluded that ice fishing was the most miserable sport ever conceived by man. After two or three hours I gave it up and went home.

It was not until much later when I finally saw a graying that I learned that they have a very small mouth. A grayling could not have swollowed the wad of bait I put down that hole no matter how much it might have wanted it. In any case, that was my one and only ice fishing experience. I've had absolutely no desire to try it since.

The assignment in Alaska proved to be a great adventure in and of itself, but there were often occasions when things did not go as planned, and we physicians referred to such events as "Great Alaska Adventures."

# A GREAT ALASKAN ADVENTURE

The Chena River separates Fairbanks from Ft. Wainwright, and in 1972 there was a road that followed the river for ten miles upstream where there was a pull-off where one could park a vehicle. The road was straight whereas the river was sinuous with large sigmoid curves, so that its length was at least thrice that of the road. It was a beautiful river of clean, clear water bordered by abundant vegetation. There is not much of an altitude drop between the pull-off and Fairbanks, so the river is considered a grade I float for canoers and kyakers—suitable for novices. That is not to say that there are no rapids—there are, and some provide a fairly stiff challenge for beginners.

I bought a 17 ft. Canoe at J. C. Penny in Fairbanks, and a surgeon, Bob Cole, and I decided it would be great fun to float the Chena. Bob had considerable experience in a canoe, but I had never been in one. After talking to others, we devised a plan to make the float. Several miles up the road toward the pull-off there was a turn-off onto a road that led to the river directly across from the Eielson AFB campground. The campground was a good landmark as there was a large open area with picnic tables near the river's edge. The plan was to drive two vehicles. I had the canoe atop mine. We would park Bob's vehicle next to the river across from Eielson and then take the canoe to the pull-off. We would have a roughly ten mile float down the river to his vehicle where we would then beach the canoe and drive his car up to the pull-off, pick up my Landcruiser and retrieve the canoe on the way back home.

Our grand scheme went awry almost from the outset. We thought the turnoff went straight to the river. Nobody told us that there was a long slough we had to bypass before we got there. Since we were anxious to begin our grand adventure, and we thought we knew what we were doing, we didn't even look at the other bank to see if there was a campground. We parked his car alongside the water and went happily on our way.

Once at the pull-off, we had to carry the canoe about a hundred yards through brush and across muskeg to get the River. It was early June and still chilly in Alaska, so we put on our jackets and pulled mosquito nets over our hats. Bob took the lead, and we hoisted the canoe over our heads. Bob had barely stepped into the muskeg when mosquitos swarmed up so thick it would have been difficult to breath had we not had the nets over our heads. By the time we had gone 50 ft. there were so many mosquitos on Bob's back I could not tell the color of his jacket. We were well protected, but I had to wonder how the old prospecters of years past had managed. The Alaskan mosquitos are not only abundant in the spring, but they are huge by mosquito standards. The gift shops all through Alaska sell mosquito replicas made of two lacquered moose turds with a toothpick for a proboscis. They call them Moosquitos. I decided that the size of the Moosquitos was not much of an exaggeration. We launched the canoe, got out onto the water, and the mosquitos gradually went away. We then were adequately protected with mosquito repellant, but it was touch and go when we pulled into shore to fish.

We had heard that the average river fisherman on foot will fish the river for three miles after leaving his vehicle. Supposedly, when you get beyond that distance, the fishing gets much better. The pull-off was used mainly by fishermen and there were, indeed, a couple of guys fishing when we arrived. We wanted to fish, but I had much to learn concerning paddling and navigating a canoe, so those first miles were usefully spent under Bob's tutelage. I was seated up front, and Bob taught me how to paddle, how to drift the boat sideways and backpaddle to get around corners and how to maneuver through rapids. Once we figured we were far enough down the river, and I was sufficiently tutored, we began to stop and fish whereever we found what looked like a promising hole. We were using light spinning line and small Mepps spinners, and we caught and released dozens of grayling. Grayling look nothing like brook trout, but they are much like brookies in that they are smallish, not very wary and relatively easy to catch. An 18 inch grayling is considered a trophy fish.

Along about mid-afternoon, we considered that we should be getting to the end of our drift, and we began watching for Bob's car. Around 4 PM we noticed a large open space with picnic tables on the left bank. It resembled what we thought the Eielson camp ground would look like, but there was no car sitting on the opposite bank. It should have been right next to the water. Somewhat confused and not knowing what else to do we continued to drift. Our anxiety levels soared as we watched hopefully for another camp ground as the miles passed by. Eventually we realized that we somehow had made a dreadful mistake but the current was swift enough that there was no way to paddle back upstream.

The only alternative appeared to be to drift all the way to Ft. Wainwright. We had no idea how long it would take, but we figured we were in for a long night. In June it does not get dark. The sun sets about 10 PM and rises at 2 AM. For four hours it will be dusky but not pitch black. Along about sundown, we saw a cluster of cabins near the river. We beached the boat and with great hope checked the cabins out. There was no one around. It appeared that the cabins had not been used all winter. We considered walking out to the highway, but we didn't know how far it was and, at that time of night, we were not sure we would be any better off. At least there were no grizzlies out in the river. We returned to the canoe and resumed our drift.

After what seemed like an eternity, the Eastern sky began to lighten and, suddenly, we heard the roar of a gasoline engine. A few moments later, a large jet propelled, flat bottomed river boat appeared from down stream, rapidly approaching. As it drew near, it slowed and pulled alongside of us. One of the two guys on board asked, "How in the hell did you guys get here?" We related our sad story. When the guys stopped laughing, they took two very tired, embarrassed and grateful canoists aboard and pulled our canoe onto the boat. They had been on the river fishing most of the night. They stopped a few places to fish, but they eventually took us to Ft. Wainwright and dropped us off just before dawn.

Bob lived the closest to the river, so we walked to his house where he was confronted by a very worried but relieved wife, and then he drove me to my house where I was greeted by a woman that was even more upset. Both wives swore that their dumbshit husbands would never set foot in the Alaskan wilderness again. At that point, we were almost inclined to agree. We both caught a few hours sleep, and then, Sunday morning, Bob's wife drove us back up the road toward the pull-off. We found Bob's car next to the slough, about a mile from the river exactly where we had left it. We verbally kicked ourselves and then retrieved my Landcruiser. Thus ended Carl's and Bob's Great Alaska Adventure.

# SALMON FISHING AT VALDEZ

We physicians were assigned to the Bassett Army Hospital at Ft. Wainwright for two year tours. We worked hard and sometimes put in long hours, but we were all determined to get as much enjoyment out of our time in Alaska as we possibly could. That being the case, we readily shared with each other our contacts and passed on information regarding our outings. Someone gave me the name of a fishing guide that worked out of Valdez.

Valdez harbor is a very large harbor in the Gulf of Alaska, and it is considered its most important port. The town of Valdez is a small community on the edge of the harbor, and its main industry prior to the Valdez Oil Pipeline was fishing. The pipeline ends at Valdez and in 1979 Valdez became known world wide when an oil tanker, the Exxon Valdez hit a reef, and there was a monunemental oil spill. Thankfully, that occurred after my time, and fishing was still the main attraction in 1971.

There are numerous rivers that empty into the harbor, and those rivers are spawning grounds for several varieties of salmon. I called the guide and learned that the pink salmon were running, so I made an appointment for my wife and I on a Saturday morning in early June of 1971. His services were rather expensive, so I scheduled only a half-day. At the appointed time, we met a wiry, middle-aged man with a deeply tanned, weathered face. He was clean shaven with a receding hairline, and he wore dark glasses. He was dressed in jeans with a long-sleeved, plaid flannel shirt. He was hatless which surprised me as he spent long hours in the sun. We learned that he spent his summers in Alaska and his winters in Montana. His boat was a diesel tub much like the ones that ran out of Westport Washington, but it was considerably smaller. About six people could fish comfortably, but on this day, Clea and I had it to ourselves.

The skipper ran the boat about half an hour across the bay and lowered the anchor in the mouth of a river where pink salmon were staging. The water looked as if it were boiling as thousands of fish broke the surface. Pink Salmon (also known as humpies) are the smallest and most abundant of the salmon species. They spend only two years in the ocean. The average weight of a Pink is 4.8 lbs., but a record catch of 15 lbs.[2] has been recorded. Because of their small size, they are amonst the least popular of the salmon from the sportsman's point of view which explained why no other boats were there. Here we were with all those fish and solitude also. How good could it get? I figured I could happily spend my life catching 5 lb. fish. They are very good to eat, and in June 1971 the limit was 15 fish.

The skipper strung up our poles and clipped onto our leaders a spoon that was red on the convex surface and shiney silver on the other. Clea and I made our first casts and WHAM! We both hooked fish right away, and our poles bent almost double. Those humpies were very strong fish. They ran, leaped, shook and ran some more. They ripped the line off our reels. We wound it back and they ripped it off again. It took several minutes, but finally we brought them to the net. We cast again, and it was the same story. We were hooking fish every cast. After Clea caught four fish her arms were aching, and she decided that she could not tolerate the no-seeums (pesky biting gnats) that were getting after her face, so she put her pole away and went into the cabin. We had insect repellant, but Clea did not like the gnats bumping her face and darting in front of her eyes. I stayed on the deck, ignored the ache in my arms, tolerated the pesky gnats and caught both of our limits before our half day expired. Who could ever have dreamed of catching 30 salmon in a half day? Man, was I tired! We returned to the dock, traded all but a few of the fish for canned salmon at the cannery, put the rest in a large cooler and headed home. We shared fish with all of our friends, and I smoked a big batch on my Little Chief Smoker.

When I bragged about our trip and shared some of the fish with a surgeon friend of mine, John Brunner, he became very excited and asked if we would go again and take him and his wife, Sue. I called the guide and made an appointment for a Saturday two weeks hence. John did the driving and I was glad he did, because he and Sue had a large, white German Shepherd that they took with us. I have no recollection of what we did with the dog while we fished, but I was doubly glad we had John's car when we made the ride home.

Once again, our appointment was for a half day. This time the guide took us to the mouth of a different river where the coho (silver) salmon were running. These salmon spend four years in the ocean and usually run 7 – 11 lbs. though they may get as large as 35 lbs.[3] They are highly popular with sportsmen. Their popularity was evident as there were boats everywhere. Our skipper found a spot a respectful distance from other boats and lowered the anchor. He put a large sinker on the end of our lines and followed that with a six foot leader with double hooks on the end which he baited with cut herring. The sinkers, it turned out, were for casting purposes as his instructions were to cast as far as we could and rapidly reel the line back in. We began to cast and retrieve, cast and retrieve, and we were catching nothing.

After about 20 minutes, I wondered what would happen if I tried fishing Westport style. I lowered my sinker to the bottom, raised it back up about six feet and started jigging it up and down. I had made only a few jigs when a fish nearly ripped the pole out of my hands. My reel began to scream, and a large silver erupted from the water and soared high into the air. It slammed back into the water and turned toward me. I reeled furiously trying to keep up and then, suddenly, the fish reversed directions and ripped out all the line I had gained. I had thought the pinks were fun to catch, but they were not even in the same league as these babies. I finally got the fish close to the boat, and the skipper scooped it into the net. He re-baited my hook, and I dropped it to the bottom again. WHAM! I was off and running. "Drop your bait to the bottom and jig it," I yelled. Soon one or the other of us had a fish on all the time or sometimes two of us had fish on at a the same time. We were running around the boat, passing our rods over or under our companions poles, trying to avoid getting our lines tangled while the fish ran whichever direction suited them. Reels were shrieking, we were hooting and laughing and having the time of our lives. The clients on the boats near us were beginning to cast as far toward us as the could. Their skippers started the big diesels and inched closer. Soon their clients were casting right next to our boat, and still they caught nothing. I was going to shout over and tell them what to do, but my skipper said, "Don't you tell them a thing." I guess there was some prestige to be had for being the only skipper catching fish.

John, Clea and I were all catching silvers, but every time Sue dropped her bait to the bottom she hooked a big halibut. It was really strange since none of the rest of us caught them. Once she managed to wrestle one of those monsters to the surface, the captain shot it in the head with a hand gun, gaffed it and, with great effort, hauled it aboard. Some of them were very large. Sue did finally manage to hook a couple of Silvers, but she was not dissatisfied with the halibut.

The limit on the Silvers was eight fish, so we soon had our limits and headed for the pier. To our great amusement, the other boats collapsed into the area we vacated so fast they nearly ran over one another.

Once again we traded most of our fish at the cannery and headed home with abundant fresh salmon and halibut filets. After some miles, we stopped at the side of the road near a wooded area to relieve ourselves (there were no rest stops). Heidi, the dog, apparently was uncomfortably warm riding in the car, so she trotted down the road to a large mud puddle and flopped down in it completely wetting her belly with filthy water. As she soaked up that cold water, she got the most contented look on her face. The puddle was about 30 feet from the car, and I've never understood why Heidi could not have shaken off the mud and water when she first arose out of the puddle. Maybe it was a bit of doggy humor, but she returned to the car, within five feet of us, and shook herself vigorously, splattering all of us with grungy water. Then she happily hopped back into the car where she deposited a nice layer of mud in the cargo area, and for miles we all got to enjoy the odor of wet dog.

# NEAR HOMICIDE ON THE COPPER RIVER

A little over three quarters of the way from Fairbanks to Valdez, there is a small settlement called Copper Center. Near Copper Center there is the origin of a 20 mile jeep road (a very rough jeep road) that follows the Copper River to Klutina Lake. The King Salmon were running up the Copper River, and I learned that very large sea-run dolly varden followed them to their spawning beds to eat their eggs. Jim Jeffers and I decided it would be a great adventure to go to Klutina Lake and test our luck at catching those big bull trout. Jim was a Texas boy and, in true Texas style, had more bullshit stories than any human I ever met. He was fun to be with. We had been told that the road into Klutina Lake was a tough drive, but that was a significant understatement. My knuckles were so white after that trip I was surprised when the color returned. We encountered places where the road was washed out, and to get past those spots I had to drive up onto the adjacent hillside. Going below the wash-out was not an option unless you wanted to take a very steep plunge into the river canyon. The hillside above was slightly less steep, and I was fearful (terrorized?) that I would roll the landcruiser. Somehow, the vehicle managed to keep all four wheels on the ground, and after each wash-out I breathed a deep sigh of relief. Jim, with infinite wisdom, got out of the car, watched until I got across those places and then walked across. I should have driven off without him.

When we got to the lake, we were surprised to find a cabin which was inhabited by a grizzly bear/moose/dall sheep guide who sometimes lived there year around, and he had spent the previous winter there. He had two male dalmatian dogs. He said he was told that those short haired dogs would never survive the winter at his camp, but they did. He said that huskies and malamutes are very territorial and won't share the holes they dig in the snow for their beds. The dalmatians, on the other hand, crawled under an overturned boat and curled up together. They not only survived, but many of the pups born in Copper Center the following spring had black and white spots. We asked him about the hunts that he guided, and he indicated that he usually had two to four hunters at a time at a cost of $1500 (in 1971) apiece for a ten day hunt. We asked him what he did with the hunters if they scored their kills right away. He laughed and said he knew every grizzly, moose and dall sheep in his territory practically by name, and he knew exactly where to find them. The trick was to lead the hunters around the wilderness for a few days, feed them well, ply them with booze in the evenings, tell stories and play cards, and then on the last three days of the hunt take them to where he knew the game would be. I thought, "Yeh, that's about what I figured."

Klutina Lake is a large body of water which is emerald green. The guide told us the green color was due to silt from a melting glacier. I suppose that is correct but, aside from the green color, the lake water was very clear. The outlet of the lake was the headwaters for the Copper River. Jim and I set up our camp, and the next day set out to fish the creeks and tributaries running into Klutina Lake. We worried a little bit about the fresh grizzly tracks along the banks, but we never did see a bear. This was fortunate because I foolishly thought the .44 magnum handgun I was carrying was good protection from bears. I later learned that a handgun probably won't stop a charging bear— even if you have time to get a shot off.

The fishing was fantastic—just throw a spoon or almost any lure that had some red color on it over the salmon redds and, WHAM, you had your fish. The limit was 10 fish. I was catching and releasing mine, but Jim was keeping everything. I said, "Jim, you need to turn those fish loose or you will limit out and have to quit fishing." He said, "OK" but the next fish he caught he'd say, "Man, look at the size of this fish. This is the biggest fish I ever caught in my life. I can't throw it back." Into his creel it would go. Soon he had his limit, but he kept fishing, and before long he had mine also, so we both had to quit. What a guy! The worst part of it all was we ended up at camp with 20 beautiful fish and we proceeded to fry up a few. They were dreadful. They tasted just like fish eggs smell.

The next morning we started the drive back to Copper Center. The water in the Klutina River was crystal clear, and a few miles down stream from the lake we could see huge King Salmon swimming upstream. We stopped and broke out our big salmon rods and rigged them up to try some snag fishing which was legal in Alaska at the time. You tied a large lead weight on the end of your line and then, just a short ways up the line, you rigged a spoon with a large treble hook. The object was to locate some salmon resting in a pool, toss the lure over the pool and then try to jerk it back across their backs. It worked! On about the third try I snagged a huge male just in front of the dorsal fin, and it took off downstream. There was no stopping it, so I started running along the bank. That fish was taking line the whole time. There was a tree in my path, and I wanted jim to hold the pole while I ran around the tree, and then hand it back to me. Instead, he reached out and grabbed the line. Snap! That was the end of that fish. If I had killed Jim I'm sure it would have been justifiable homicide. He consoled me with, "You'd have never landed him anyway." Try as we might, we could not snag another fish.

We drove the jeep road back and sure enough about ten miles from Copper Center we passed a dalmatian, red tongue hanging out, hightailing it back to camp.

# FISHING WITH DAD IN ALASKA

When Clea and I married we thought we'd run as a twosome for a year, and then begin the process of raising a family. To our surprise and distress, when we began trying to have kids nothing happened, so in June, 1971, Clea and I adopted an infant girl we named Marlisa. The baby needed to be named and blessed, but Clea and I had not set foot in the church since our arrival in Alaska, so we asked Mom and Dad if they could make the trip to Alaska, so Dad could do the honors. In early August Mom and Dad flew into Fairbanks, and the following Sunday Dad named and blessed our baby. Just as I had when they visited me in Tacoma, I took a week of leave, and we had a teriffic vacation.

Some months earlier I had bought a camp trailer from a departing NCO. It was merely an 8'X8' box, but it was rather cleverly arranged. Near the door on the right side there was an ice box sitting next to a small propane stove. The ice box had shelves for food, but if you put enough ice in it to do any good there was little room for either food or beverage. On the left side was a small cabinet and wash basin that drained into a 5 gallon bucket. Over the wheel wells on both sides there were bench type seats with a table in between. The table cleverly folded out of the way, and the seats became beds. Collapsible frames could be unfolded and suspended over each bench creating two more hammock type beds, so the trailer would sleep four.

We hooked the trailer onto our Landcruiser, and set out for Denali National Park. The weather was good, and we did most of our cooking and eating outside. At night Mom and Dad slept on the benches, and Clea and I slept on the hammocks. Marlisa was in a basket on the floor. We managed very comfortably, and we slept in safety from bears and other wild life. This was very comforting as all the camp sites had bear warnings posted. In Denali we saw wild life of just about every kind, and we saw occasional tourists that were very foolish in the risks they took to get pictures of Grizzlies, but they were lucky and sustained no harm.

On our way home we traveled the Denali Highway. Midway between Mt. McKinnely and Fairbanks there was a gas station, store and a lodge—fittingly called the Denali Lodge. About mid-afternoon we stopped there, gassed up and continued on our way. We had traveled only a few miles when we were overtaken by a vehicle that pulled close behind us an began honking its horn. I pulled over to see what the fuss was. The driver pointed out that a cross beam on my trailer had broken and was almost dragging the highway. Yikes! We thanked him profusely and slowly returned to the lodge. The people in Alaska are extra-ordinarily friendly and go way out of their way to be helpful. A mechanic at the lodge pointed out that I needed a welder to make my repair. There was no welder on site, but I was informed that there was a hermit off in the hills that could do the work. It would be necessary to send a messenger to his cabin—and hope that he was home. In any case, nothing would be done until the next day. We decided to spend a night in the comfort of the lodge.

We were eating dinner about 6 PM when a bush pilot walked through the door of the lodge carrying a long stringer of grayling and lake trout. I heard him tell the manager that he had flown two geologists into a small lake that he ordinarily flew past when he was carrying clients. He landed on the lake, and while the Geologists were doing their work, he decided to see what the fishing was like. He had stood on the float of his plane and caught fish every cast. I walked over, admired the fish, and asked him what he would charge to fly Dad and me to that lake and leave us a few hours. His eyebrows raised in surprise. "Now," he asked? "Yes," I replied. He thought it over for a few moments and then, with an amused look on his face, said he said he would do it for $60 apiece as soon as he refueled his plane. I about tore my pocket off I got my wallet out so fast. I handed him the cash and Dad and I raced to the trailer for our gear. It was early August in Alaska—past the summer solstice but close enough that, although it got dusky, it still did not get dark at night.

The pilot was an affable fellow and the short flight pleasant. We landed on the lake about 8 PM. The pilot left and Dad and I slathered ourselves with mosquito repellant and began to fish. Just as the pilot had, we caught grayling or lake trout every cast. I don't think those fish had ever seen a fisherman. I had always thought lake trout were deep water fish. I suppose this lake may have been deep in the middle but it didn't look it. Never-the-less, lake trout were present in abundance all over the lake, though they were not very large by lake trout standards. They were, however, somewhat larger than the grayling, and the grayling were truly trophy sized. We started switching spinners and other lures to see how many things we could get the fish to take. They took everything we threw out. Talk about spending quality time with your father!

About 2 AM the pilot returned and flew us back to Denali. He flew much farther than he had to so as to point out moose, caribou and huge flocks of water fowl. It seemed as if every beast and bird was moving as dawn flooded over the muskeg. It was almost as if the muskeg itself was in motion. I'd never seen so much wild life. It was truly spectalular. I have reflected many times on the kindness of the pilot, but he seemed to thoroughly enjoy showing us that great land. Not only did he go out of his way to show the wild life to us he stayed up almost all night to accommodate two vacationing greenhorns all for $120. Never was vacation money better spent.

The following day a long haired, bearded, elderly fellow arrived out of the bush to fix our trailer. He was unkempt, his clothes filthy and he was missing some teeth but he was friendly, and he knew how to weld. There is no trash service in the interior of Alaska and, because of the permafrost, no trash is buried. Most cabins and other dwellings have a trash pile out back. He needed a piece of angle iron to make the repair, and he obtained it by cutting the side off an old army cot that was on the trash heap. He made the fix and I later came to realize that the trailer was sturdier and better than it had been before. As with the bush pilot, his charges were very reasonable, and my gratitude to him profound.

We returned home and I had another trip lined up for Dad and me. I knew another bush pilot that had a cabin at a place called Minto Flats. When he built it, he had flown sheets of plywood to the site by tying them to the wing struts. I cannot imagine flying a small plane with an 8x4 sheet of plywood tied under each wing, but those guys seemed to be able to fly anything. I arranged for an overnight trip at his cabin, and he flew us in. Minto Flats was reputed to be a great place for catching great northern pike. Unfortunately, it had rained for several days before we made our trip, and the water was high and muddy. We went anyway. I had never fished for pike, but I read a lot about it and bought wire leaders and what I thought were appopriate lures. We caught nothing which I suppose should have been predictable since the water conditions were far less than optimal and neither Dad nor I knew what we were doing.

Since we we were catching no fish we decided to kill some time target shooting with my .44 magnum pistol. We set up a target and backed off a hundred feet or so. I shot first. I assumed a two handed stance with my arms extended and my elbows locked. I fired off two rounds and then handed the pistol to Dad. He held it with both hands, but he had the weapon about four inches from his face. I said, "Uh—Dad. You better extend your arms and lock your elbows." Indignantly he replied, "I know how to shoot a pistol!" "O. K." I said with reluctance. Dad fired off a round, and that cannon kicked backward and upward. The hammer peeled off a quarter inch wide strip of skin extending from the middle of his nose to the top of his forehead. "OH HELLY," he screamed. He shoved the gun back into my hands and grabbed his nose. I almost collapsed to the ground laughing, but I managed to choke out, "I tried to tell you." Sheepishly he confessed, "I had no idea anything could kick like that." In any case, he would not fire it again and I was truly glad the kick back did not smash his nose.

Dad is the only person I have ever known that said, "Oh helly." After Clea and I got married he and mom visited us in Tacoma. Dad walked out on the dock at our place, stepped on a spot slick with moss and slipped down. When he got up, he saw that he had green goop smeared all down the side of his pants. His comment was, "Oh helly I'm a mess." To this day Clea and I repeat that when our clothing gets soiled.

As with all things, the vacation ended far too soon and Mom, with her journal and Dad, with the linear scab on his nose were homeward bound from a trip they would never forget and I was back at work.

# ALASKAN MOSQUITOS

Mosquitos in the Alaskan interior are big, and they are ferocious. Worse yet, they are abundant. Spring and summer temperatures thaw only the top few inches of the soil and below that is permafrost. Since the melting snow water has no place to sink large marshes form which the locals call muskeg and niggerheads. In the midst of the boggy areas (muskeg) large clumps of grass grow from decomposing vegetation (niggerheads). When wishing to cross a swampy area one is tempted to try it by stepping on the niggerheads, but if your intent is to stay high and dry you will be sadly disappointed as the clumps bend sideways, and you get dumped into the standing water. These areas are perfect breeding grounds for mosquitos, and in the spring, as soon as the temperature is above freezing and the top layer of soil starts to thaw mosquitos are present in droves. Fortunately, they diminish in late summer, and in the fall, after a hard frost, they essentially disappear.

Mosquito repellant was an essential item for anyone venturing anywhere near the muskeg. The stuff issued in olive drab squeeze bottles by the military was far superior to Off and other commercial brands in terms of keeping mosquitos away, but since it was not issued in spay cans it had to be squeezed into your palm and liberally smeared onto areas you wished to protect. It was necessary to be cautious in applying it to the face. If you got it into your eye it burned like fire. It had one other potentially distressing side effect. It disolved plastic. Getting it onto plastic frames or lenses of eyeglasses resulted in a huge aggravation. The frames might show only an unsightly distorted spot, but lenses became permanently fogged. I learned of its effect on plastic when I had some residual on my hands when I started to fish. The handle on my reel was plastic and I soon found my thumb and first finger stuck to it—almost like super glue. I pulled them free and the handle rehardened, but it forever had my fingerprints embedded into it. It was not a good idea to handle your fishing line or leader if you had that stuff on your hands. On top of everything else, it stunk. I'm relatively sure that fish didn't much care for the smell of it either.

Because of the distasteful aspects of using the repellant, I was overjoyed when I walked into J. C. Penny in Fairbanks and saw a shelf of small devices about the size of a modern small cell phone. They were supposed to repel mosquitos. The accompanying literature said to just clip the device onto your belt and, when turned on, it would emit a high pitched sound (too high to be detected by the human ear) which would keep mosquitos away. I bought one each for Clea and me, and we ventured out into the cool of the evening to give them a test. We turned them on, but there was no way to tell whether or not they were actually doing anything. How do you detect a sound too high pitched to hear? We quickly learned that the only way those devices had an effect on mosquitos was if you took it in your hand and used it to squash one that was already sucking blood. Those things were like a lot of fishing lures—designed to hook the guy bearing a wallet but otherwise ineffective.

The back area of Ft. Wainwright was wild country. There was an unpaved road that extended into an area where there were abundant ponds and sloughs. There were numerous decidual trees that reflected off the water, and on windless days the scenic beauty was enough to make a landscape artist's heart beat faster. I first went back there in early September to shoot ducks. We had already had a hard frost so there were no mosquitos, and the folliage on the trees had turned from green to hues of yellow and red. I was eager to see if there were any fish in all that water so I launched my canoe. To my great disappointment there seemed to be no fish at all, but the wide sloughs turned out to be an excellent place to practice J-stroking and other paddling techniques. It was so peaceful I fell in love with the place.

The following spring I eagerly returned thinking to enjoy the solitude of the place and practice my canoing prior to going out on the river. There had been no mosquitoes on my previous trip, and I had not given them a thought. I parked my Landcruiser and stepped out onto the grass. As soon as my foot hit the ground a cloud of mosquitos swarmed around me. I took a couple of steps, and with each one the cloud got thicker. By the time I got to the front of my vehicle I was covered with mosquitos and I couldn't breath without inhaling them. I turned and beat a hasty retreat back into the car. Refuge was not complete since I now had a car full of mosquitoes. I fled the area and stopped the first place I came to that looked dry. I opened all the doors allowing the trapped mosquitoes to escape. I managed to get rid of

most of them but I had plenty of wheals and whelts to remember them
by. Strangely, my love for that idyllic place diminished, and I never
went back.

# HOME AGAIN, HOME AGAIN

My Tour in Alaska ended in June, 1972, and I was reassigned to the Madigan Army Medical Center where I became a member of the teaching staff. Once again I was assigned housing in the Beachwood area at Ft. Lewis just a stone's throw from American Lake. Clea's parents lived in Lake City, near Tacoma, so we had the advantage of loving grandparents living nearby to dote on Marlisa. I learned that one of life's greatest blessings was to have in-laws that actually liked me. We spent a lot of time together, and Clea's dad, Harold, frequently went out of his way to be helpful to me. If I were going to be doing a project Clea would casually mention it to her mom. The next thing I knew her dad would show up prepared to help. We had a wonderful relationship.

One Saturday afternoon my in-laws were at our house, and my mother-in-law stood looking out over American Lake. The water was sky-blue and there was just a light riffle from the wind. Part of the lake on the shore opposite Ft. Lewis was bordered by homes, and most of those homes were quite spectacular. There was a nice sand beach at Tillicum and another really lovely beach across the lake at a public park. In many places there were decidual trees extending to the waterline. A couple of hydroplanes were ripping up and down the main lake, and here and there small groups of young people were water skiing. One such group was skiing off the gravel beach just below our house. It was an idyllic scene. My mother-in-law began to wax poetic about how much she had loved to fish when she was a girl. I jokingly asked how she'd like to get out on American Lake and drown a worm. I was only mildly surprised when she asked, "How soon can we go?" I could see no better time than the present.

There was a crude launch area near my house, so I backed my boat down to the water's edge and put on my waders. The launch area was unpaved, and it was necessary to go into the water to pull the boat off the trailer. I knew I'd need my waders to get the boat back onto the trailer, so I just left them on while we fished.

I've had a life long problem passing kidney stones. I was a sophomore in medical school when I passed the first one, and for many years I passed three or four every year. Back then the best treatment was to stay well hydrated. In order to do that I drank a lot of water, and what goes in one end comes out the other. Whenever I took long car trips with my family, my wife and kids never had to ask for rest stops. The kids could outlast me about three stops to one. This was well known and something of a family joke.

Arba and I were on the lake all afternoon. The fishing was good, and we had caught and released numerous rainbow trout. She was sitting on the transom and mostly watching her line behind the boat. Whenever I had to pee, I had a small can that I dropped down into my waders, and Arba was completely unaware. Late in the evening and about the third time I had used the can she caught me pulling it out of my waders. She let out a loud guffaw, and then laughed until tears ran down her face. I thought she was going to fall off the back of the boat. When she could finally get a few words out she said, "Damn you Carl. My teeth have been floating for the past two hours, and I didn't say anything because I was sure I could outlast you." Well, when you fish with women, you have to be just a little bit wily.

# THE PORCUPINE LAKES

By the time I had been back from Alaska for a year, I was getting a hankering to do some kind of a *real* fishing trip. I had been to Westport a time or two, but the salmon limits off the Washington coast had been cut to two fish. After the 8-15 fish limits in Alaska, the run to Westport hardly seemed worth the trip. Clea and I had become good friends with one of the pathology residents, Jerry Rappe and his wife, Chris. The more we talked about fishing the better the idea of some kind of fishing safari sounded. I found some ads for outfitters working out of the Challis, Idaho area. I selected one at random and made a call. My call was taken by a woman who said her husband had recently died, and she was going to try to run his business. Of the possibilities that she offered, a trip to a group of three lakes called the Porcupine Lakes located in the Idaho wilderness area sounded like just the ticket, and her string was available just when we wanted to go.

Clea, Chris, Jerry and I made the 1200 mile trip to Challis in my Landcruiser and, following the outfitter's directions, found ourselves, very early in the morning, in a isolated piece of desert wondering if we had misunderstood the instructions. There was a creek running through the valley which was the only suggestion of possible fish life, and it was bordered by a strip of green plant life and a few willows. Aside from that the area was bone dry with sagebrush as the dominant vegetation for many miles. This did not look promising, but soon a couple of large trucks joined us and two wranglers began unloading horses and mules. Introductions were made, and they soon had the pack animals loaded with equipment, the riding horses saddled, and we were off. I was seated aboard a bay mare that turned out to be a pretty good horse. We started out on a trail that basically followed the creek but was just far enough away to forego any benefits from the moisture. I was at the end of the line, and the trail dust stirred up by the animals ahead soon had me enveloped in a thick cloud of dust. It's never a good idea to be in the dust eating position. The one benefit from my place at the end of the line was being able to see what was going on up ahead. There were prickly pear cacti alongside the trail and, to my utter amazement, one of the pack mules kept reaching down and snatching a mouthful as he walked by. The spines on those things were three quarters of an inch long, and they seemed not to affect the mule in the least. He chewed away like he had a mouth full of grass, and if he was taking any precautions with those spines it was inapparent to me. He'd swallow his mouthful, and at the next opportunity reach down and grab another. How could any critter's mouth be that tough? A human would have had to use thick leather gloves and special precautions to harvest those things, but I have heard that they are good to eat. I've seen jars of Prickly Pear Cactus Jelly in stores.

After a few miles we began to gain elevation and entered into pine forest. By then I was coated with dust, and there were wet circles of mud around my eyes and my mouth. The dust diminished drastically to my relief, and the scenic beauty increased just as drastically. The creek became a series of rapids with cool, clear water tumbling over small waterfalls into crystal pools. The visual beauty and the magical sound of running, falling water made me want to hop off my mare and check out the fishing. Since that was not an option, we continued onward, but the ride had now become very pleasant—if one ignored tender bottoms that were beginning to get sore.

Finally we passed the lower of the three lakes and were mesmerized by the translucent water. You could easily see the bottom of the lake and virtually everything in there. I was now getting really excited to start fishing. A couple of miles later we rode past the middle lake, and about a half mile after that we reached the camp at the upper lake. A large wall tent was already in place with a table in the center. Camp chairs were arranged around a fire pit, and there was even a wooden privy. We were going to camp in comfort. We expected the wranglers to unload our stuff and ride back down the mountain, but the two young men, both around age twenty, said their boss had told them to stay put until time for us to leave. Once our gear was unloaded, the young men tied a chase horse to a tree, hobbled the other horses and mules and allowed them to go free to forage. They warned us that the fishing might not be up to par as a week previously a large troop of boy scouts had camped on the lake, fished heavily and kept everything they caught. To our disappointment, that prediction turned out to be true. The fishing was a little slow. Never-the-less we caught some nice sized brook trout that, coming from that crystal clear, cold water, were absolutely wonderful to eat. I've never eaten better fish.

Since the fishing was a little slow at the upper lake, Jerry Rappe and I decided to hike a half mile or so down to the middle lake and check it out. We were using spinning rods with Mepp spinners, and as soon as we arrived at the lake, Jerry walked to onto an embankment at the lake's edge. He did not realize that it had been undercut by the water. He swung his pole with a heave sufficient to cast that spinner half way to the moon, and as he shifted his weight to his front foot the bank collapsed from underneath him. By the time he hit the water his feet were churning so fast he looked like an egg beater. While turning the air blue with ear blistering language, he scurried back up the bank with such speed he hardly got his feet wet. I was convulsing with laughter. When I finally got myself under control I told Jerry I now believed that a man could walk on water—I'd just seen it done.

When the time came to break camp we decided that we would stop at the lower lake on the way out and try the fishing there for a couple of hours. Jerry, Chris and I stashed our spinners in our tackle boxes, broke down our poles and placed them in their carrying cases. Clea did not. She kept her pole intact, left it strung up with the lure hooked into the lowest eyelet, and just held the pole close alongside her horse to keep it from snagging in the trees.

The trail passed right along the edge of the lower lake, and as we rode near we could see a deep hole about 20 feet off shore, and in that hole a few dozen brookies were resting—almost perfectly still. We all leaped off our horses, and Jerry, Chris and I scrambled for our rod cases. Clea simply walked to the water's edge and made a cast. "I got one," she sang out almost as soon as her spinner hit the water. She was loath to touch a fish, so she never would unhook her own. By the time I got my rod out of the case, she had that wildly flailing fish dangling in front of my face. I dropped everything and quickly unhooked the fish. She made another cast and said, laughingly, "I've got another one." By the time I had my pole strung up, she had that one in front of my face. I unhooked it and started frantically trying to separate the mepp spinners which were now a tangled mess in my tackle box. I finally separated one and started to tie it on. I had the knot about half finished when Clea dangled another frantic brookie before my eyes.

I let go of the knot and unhooked the fish. I had to start the knot all over again, and just as I was ready to make a cast Clea slapped me alongside the head with still another flopping fish . As I unhooked that fish Clea announced, "That's enough." She set her pole down alongside the trail, plopped her butt down onto the dirt, leaned back against the embankment, pulled a book out of her pocket and started to read. I was astounded. Then I looked out into the hole she had been fishing and there was nary a fish to be seen. She'd spooked them all away.

Jerry, Chris and I made a dozen or so casts without so much as a strike. I decided to walk around the lake. As I walked up to the water's edge on the other side, I saw a large brookie resting beside a log. I cast just a few feet behind him, and as soon as the spoon hit the water he whirled and shot toward it. He hit that spoon and the end of my line so hard it propelled him out of the water. He splashed back with a tremendous belly flop and began frantically tugging. He tried running straight away from me, to each side and downward, but he was mine. I caught three or four more fish and then rejoined the group to continue the ride. I don't think Jerry or Chris caught anything. As we mounted our horses I incredulously said to Clea, "How in the world can you catch four fish on four casts and then just quit?" She smiled and repeated, "Four was enough."

In the winter time, Clea and I occasionally drove to Crystal Mountain to ski. Just a few miles from Fort Lewis there was a small lake with a nearby tackle shop alongside the road, and we always passed it going and coming. Every time I saw it, I wondered about the fishing. One summer evening, I decided to quit wondering and find out. I drove to the lake, parked near the tackle shop and blew up my rubber raft. I then went into the store and asked what kind of fish were in the lake. The proprietor replied, "crappie." Crappie? I'd never heard of crappie. I asked, "What do you use to catch them?" "Crappie flies," he replied, and he led me to a case of small, white flies. I was not a fly fisherman. I was standing there with a spinning rod in my hands. The guy handed me a casting bubble and told me how to use it. I filled the bubble about ¾ full of water and slid it onto my monofilament line. I tied a small swivel to the end of my line so the bubble could not slide down onto my leader. I finished off with a six foot leader with one of those white flies tied to the end. Man, with that casting bubble I could throw that fly a hundred feet.

I paddled onto the lake and began to fish. I cast time after time after time and I caught nothing. I paddled all over that lake and still had no success. I thought I'd really been had by the guy who sold me those flies. I was about to quit fishing, but I had not yet left the water when the sun began to set. Suddenly, a crappie slammed that fly. With the setting of the sun it was as if someone had thrown a switch. That calm, smooth water was soon boiling with rising crappie, and I caught those little beggars almost every cast until it was too dark to fish. That was my introduction to crappie and it was the first time I had ever caught fish on a fly. Over the ensuing years, I have fished for crappie many times and with a variety of flies. In most lakes the best time to catch them is when they are spawning. Although evening hours are usually the best it is not always necessary to fish for them in the evenings, but at that lake, at that time the evening was where it was at.

# THE SPOKANE YEARS

In July of 1974, I had completed my payback time for all the training I had received from the army, and I decided to give civilian life a try. It was a hard decision because by then I had 12 years in the service—just eight short of retirement—and the army had been very good to me. I found what looked like a good position with a group in Spokane, Washington, however, and we ended up spending the next seven years there. Spokane is a beautiful city in Eastern Washington near the Idaho Panhandle. Water abounds, and it is said that there are 70 lakes within two hours drive from Spokane. I don't know if that is quite true or if I have remembered accurately what was said, but in any case, there is a lot of water to be fished. If one wishes big water there is Lake Coeur d' Alene, Lake Pond d' Oreille and Priest Lake in the Idaho panhandle, and all are within an easy drive.

I had sold my boat before I left Tacoma, so I spent most of my fishing time and had my greatest success on smaller lakes. I still had my canoe and a large six man rubber raft both of which I propelled with a small electric trolling motor. I preferred fishing from the rubber raft, but one winter I rolled it up and stored it on a shelf in the garage. I had caught a lot of fish, and I'm sure the bottom and side panels were abundantly saturated with fish smell. A pair of mice seemed to think so. When spring rolled around and I unrolled my boat, I discovered that a huge portion of a side panel and a goodly portion of the bottom had been chewed away, and there was a huge mouse nest. Bon apetite you little shits. Much of the chewed up rubber had been used for bedding. That seemed like a choice almost as bad as trying to eat it. I guess it was soft, but I didn't think it would do much toward absorbing the pee from baby mice. I hoped all of them had spent their time wet and miserable. It seemed like a stupid choice even for a mouse, but the raft was ruined and I was ticked.

Williams Lake, near the town of Cheney, is a short drive from Spokane, and when I wanted to fish a couple of hours after work I frequently went there. It was very small and not very scenic, but it was usually well stocked, and I could count on catching a few trout, especially after I learned where they were likely to hang out. The first couple of times I went there I trolled here and there all over the lake, but it finally dawned on me that every time I made a pass through a section of the lake near the far end I caught fish. I never did figure out what held them there, but thereafter as soon I put my boat in the water I headed directly to that area and I had excellent success.

On one camping trip we made shortly after we moved to Spokane, I had something of an epiphany. As a general rule, I do not fish on Sunday, but on this trip I made an exception. I had fished the lake of our destination on Saturday without much luck, and it left my fishing lust completely unfulfilled. There was a small creek with a beaver dam that was not far away, and we were not far from home, so I decided to try a little creek fishing on Sunday morning before we packed up. I arose at dawn well before Clea and the kids were awake and drove to the creek.

I was standing on the bank of that beaver pond, feeling a little bit guilty about being out fishing on the Sabbath, when the sun arose over the mountain. At first there was a rim of orange with a gorgeous red hue extending into the sky. Then the sunlight began to reflect off the mountains, and bright, colored surfaces were offset with deep shadows. The air was perfectly still and there was not so much as a ripple on the water, and suddenly, the sun was reflecting off the water, and the glorious colors were spreading in all directions. I had never seen anything more beautiful in my life. I asked myself, "How could anyone witness a spectacular event such as this and behold the beauty of this planet and not believe in God?" I began pondering His glorious creation, and it occurred to me that I felt far more spiritual standing near this pond with a fishing pole in my hands and witnessing this beautiful sunrise than I had ever felt sitting in church. Clea later informed me that, spiritual feeling or not, I was not going to be skipping church to fish on Sunday. That deeply religious feeling did not leave me the entire morning though I did continue to fish and I caught a few brookies.

One incident entertained me highly. Crystal, clear water spilled over the beaver dam into a small, deep pool. I dropped my worm baited hook into the pool, and a small, nine inch brookie immediately swam out from under the edge of the dam and headed toward it. Just as I thought he was going to grab it, he whirled and sped hastily away.

The cause of his retreat became apparant when a large, sixteen inch brookie zipped up from the depths and grabbed the worm. He did the little fish a huge favor by dominating the hole and grabbing all the food that day. I caught the boss. It was the largest fish I caught that trip. He was, by the way, quite delicious.

Cerlew Lake near Republic Washington became one of our favorite camping destinations. There were cabins there, and we usually rented one of them instead of taking a tent. Much of the lake was shallow, but there were some deeper areas, and the water was clean and clear. There were some very large trout in that lake, and I was determined I was going to catch one. I would see them here and there, but for the most part they were far too wary to be caught by the likes of me. They didn't get big by being dumb. I did catch a number of smaller fish, but it was the hope of catching one of those big guys that kept me coming back.

One day I was sitting at the rear of the rubber raft with one hand on my little trolling motor. I had the handle of my pole down in the raft, and I was holding it a couple of feet up the shaft, and I was trolling a large pop gear. It had been slow fishing, but I was completely content, very relaxed, and I was day dreaming. Suddenly my pole was given a vicious jerk. The handle flew up out of the raft and whacked me under the chin, nearly knocking me out of the boat. A huge trout flew out of the water, belly flopped back and snapped my line. I saw it swimming away dragging my pop gear. I got a huge rush of adrenalin, but my disappointment was almost as great as it was the time I lost my pop gear as a boy scout. It was not fitting for a grown man to cry, but rats, I never did hook another big trout, but when I got home I ripped all that 6 lb. test monofilament line off my reel and replaced it with 8 lb. test.

On one trip there was a forest fire that was not too distant. A helicopter with a huge bucket hanging from cables on the bottom kept returning to the lake, swooping down, dropping the bucket into the water and then flying off with the device filled. I wondered how it could lift all that weight, and I marveled at the skill of the pilot. It seemed to me that the huge bucket could soon empty that small lake. I hoped it was not carrying off any of those big fish.

The pathology group I worked with covered the Kootnai Memorial Hospital in Coeur d' Alene, Idaho, so I became familiar with that beautiful area. Clea and I marveled at spectacular Coeur d' Alene Lake. Where the city borders the lake there are numerous lake front homes and summer cabins. We booked a cruise on the lake one evening, and I all but drooled over those homes when I saw them from the water. "Man," I thought, "How nice it would be to spend your weekends in one of those!"

Sometime later, the family and I made a trip to Deep Lake near North Port, Washington. We camped next to a guy with a pick-up camper. In chatting with him I learned that he had owned a home on Lake Coeur d' Alene, but he sold it and bought the camper. He said that with the home he had to hustle from Spokane to Coeur d' Alene every Friday evening to prepare for the weekend guests that would invariably arrive. Then he had to hang around until late Sunday evening to clean up and haul away the trash. Moreover, with that expensive cabin he was obligated to use it, and that meant always returning to the same site. He was happy with the camper—no preparation for guests, no cleaning up after guests, and he could go camp whereever he wanted. He completely changed my thinking on owning a cabin. Years later, when the time came, I opted for a 5th wheel camper instead.

There was a tackle shop at Deep Lake, so Friday evening I browsed around looking over what they had. Hanging on the wall I found a neat looking, distinctive, red lure which was outrageously expensive, but I bought it anyway. Saturday morning I was on the water early, and I decided to see if that new lure would actually catch fish. I had not trolled far when I had a strike that nearly tore the pole out of my hands. The fish got into the weeds and broke my line, and my expensive new lure was gone. Around noon I was walking on the dock past a boat that had just pulled in from the lake. The fishermen were talking to a guy standing on the dock. One of them held up a large fish and, laughingly, said, "I caught this beauty and look what was in its lip." He held up that distinctive lure. "Hey," I said, laughing, "That's my lure." The fisherman looked at me incredulously and the corner of his mouth drew down in a, "Yeh, *sure* it is look." I told them it was I who had hooked that fish and lost the lure, but they just thought I was full of shit. One thing was for sure; It was my lure no longer.

While in Spokane, Clea and I had built for us a beautiful custom home. I had bought 49 acres of forested land near the Dishman Hills

Game Preserve. Quail, deer and coyotes in our front yard were not uncommon (and neither were mice). One summer we rented a cabin at Crescent Lake near the canadian border. The cabin was—well—rustic. The fishing was terrible, but it was such a beautiful place we thoroughly enjoyed our stay.

We had a picnic basket we always toted with us when we camped. It contained paper plates, cups, paper towels and other assorted items including snack items like jerky and cookies. We never unpacked it when we got home. When we were preparing to leave the house, we just peeked in and replaced whatever needed replentishing. When we returned home from this trip, I hurriedly toted our picnic basket into the basement and placed it in the food storage room.

A couple of weeks later I went into the basement to get a food item. I stopped dead in my tracks and did a double take. There were mouse turds all over the shelves and holes chewed in food bags. I just didn't see how it could be possible. That house was built so tight we had to crack a window to use the fire place. I started looking around, and when I opened the picnic basket I had my answer. Hitchhikers! I had toted the little beggars right in. It hadn't taken them long to start a family, either. They had chewed up the roll of paper towels, and made a huge nest which was now home to a whole raft of hairless, blind, ugly baby mice. I didn't see anything cute about them. Moreover, those adult mice had been busy. They had about two winter's worth of supplies including wheat, ramen noodles and anything else they could pack into those puffy little cheeks. I pondered how to get rid of them.

When I was a youngster, mice used to get into the old house I grew up in all the time. I slept in the basement, and the mice would get into the spaces between the floor joists, and I could lay in bed and hear them running around on the sheet rock ceiling above my head. My mother used to give me a nickel for every one I trapped. It kept me in candy money (a candy bar was $.o5 back then). Man, when I was in my room and heard one of those traps snap it was the greatest sound in the world. Now I was trying to decide whether to trap the mice or put down some Deacon. I decided on the Deacon since I would not be around to enjoy the snap of the traps. I made it easy for them. I opened a box and put it right with their food store. Two days later I went to the basement and found that there were now green mouse turds all over the place. Yep. They got it. It took me a while to find the dead adults and I threw them in the garbage. I fed the babies to the cat who was extremely appreciative, and I cleaned up the mess. I had to throw out everything in the picnic basket and spray it down with clorox water. It took me a long time to clean up the food storage area, and I had to throw out a lot of otherwise good food. Those two little beggars did a lot of damage. We were much more careful after that about checking out the stuff we returned to storage after a camp out.

Clea and I never hesitated to take the kids camping with us. We took them all from the time they were infants. Only one time did we have regrets. One beautiful July day in 1980 Clea and I decided to go camping at a small lake about two hours north of Spokane. We had been there once before and knew it was a great place for the kids to play. We loaded our camp gear, packed up the car, buckled Marlisa and Randy into their seats, placed Amy and Emery, then just over a year old, into their infant seats and took off.

We were about half way there when we heard the unmistakeable explosive release of gas and air, and after a bit an unbelievable stench filled the car. Emery had favored us with a first class blowout. In those days, disposeable diapers were not yet common, so she had on a cloth diaper and rubber pants. Liquid feces exceeded what the diaper and rubber pants could contain and it ran down her leg soiling her rompers. I had to pull off the road so we could adequately clean her up. She did not seem sick, so we assumed it was an isolated incident and continued on our way. Not to be left out, this unpleasant incident was duplicated by Amy a short time later. Perplexed, I once again pulled over and helped Clea with the clean-up. We considered returning home, but both girls seemed happy and healthy and we were almost to the camp ground, so while pondering what in the world could have set them off, we forged ahead.

We were perplexed that both girls were affected, but we still figured it was probably a one time incident. That notion was soon dispelled, and we pulled off the road yet again. Since we were then almost to the camp ground we figured we'd tough it out, and we stoically forged ahead in a car that smelled like a cess pool. Randy and Marlisa covered their faces and, amidst giggles, made a big fuss about the smell. We arrived at the camp ground, and I began the process of setting up the tent. Clea put down a blanket for the girls, and all the kids were playing and seemed perfectly well. I cheerfully assumed that the diarrhea either was, or soon would be, behind us and all would be well. We had a large wall tent that took some effort to erect, but after an hour or so I had it set up, the cots placed and all the sleeping bags arranged. In another hour, I had a dining fly strung from the trees, and I had the camp stove and the coleman lantern placed on the camp table. Everything was set for a wonderful camping experience, so I started pumping up my rubber raft. Clea, in the midst of changing another dirty diaper, gave me a "your not going fishing and leaving me with this mess" evil eye, so I pushed the raft aside and went to her aid. It was almost dinner time anyway.

We managed to get through dinner and eventually went to bed, again convinced that our problem was behind us. Just as we were almost to sleep we heard the unmistakeable THTHTHTHTHTHTHTH of a diaper being filled. For half the night one or the other of us had to sleepily crawl out of bed and attend to a problem. At midnight we were both awake. Clea changed Emery and announced that she had now used all the rompers and night clothes she had brought for the girls for the entire week, and the diaper supply was close to exhausted.

When a baby in those days filled a cloth diaper it was removed, the turds shaken out into a toilet, and the soiled diaper rinsed and tossed into a pail of clorox water. When several were accumulated they were put into the washing machine and washed. We had no pail, no clorox and no detergent, and there was no way we could launder that mess in a pristine lake. What we had was a large plastic bag filled with shitty diapers and another filled with soiled rompers. It was obvious that we were going to have to return home.

Morning finally arrived, and we downed a cold breakfast. With great frustration and considerable grumbling, I repacked all the camping equipment, rolled the sleeping bags, took down the tent, crammed all the gear back into the car. We changed amy's and Emery's diapers, strapped the kids back into their seats, and we headed home. Amy and Emery did not have a single incident of diarrhea on the way home and, in fact, neither of them crapped again for nearly two days.

I always wanted to fly fish but I didn't know how. It occurred to me that learning to tie flies would be a good way to spend some time during the winter, and I might make some connections to learn the fine art of fly casting. I learned the name of a guy named Everett who was purported to teach fly tying. Accepting his credentials entirely on faith, I gave Everett a call and enrolled for a series of weekly fly tying lessons. On the appointed Wednesday evening, following the directions I had been given, I found myself floundering around in the snow in one of the older sections of Spokane. I stumbled around in the dark trying to see house numbers and finally located the address. It was a large two room log cabin. I knocked on the door and was greeted by a moderately obese, clean shaven, white man with a thick head of greying brown hair. He was wearing a green and black, plaid wool shirt, brown felted trousers held up with wide suspenders and brown logger's boots. He peered at me over the reading glasses he had perched on the end of his nose, shook my hand and welcomed me into the house. He spoke with a melodic lilt that suggested he was not a Washington native and directed me into his classroom which was surprisingly spacious.

The whole room, literally half of the cabin, was filled with a large table surrounded by folding chairs. Near each seat was a fly tying vice and bags of feathers, hair, yarn and other supplies. Ev, as we called him, taught fly tying in that one room and lived and slept in the other. In the center of his living quarters was a large, pot-bellied wood stove which was the heat source for the entire house. The fly tying room was heated to some small degree by leaving the door open. Ev was a man of simple means. He was fly fishing's version of a ski bum. He made a few dollars by teaching fly tying and selling rods, reels and fly tying supplies to his students during the winter and spent all the time he could on the water in the summer. He lived alone and was happy to make just enough to support his fishing.

Within a few minutes the classroom filled with guys of varying ages all dressed to keep warm in the chilly room. I wondered how they had known to do that. Nobody had alerted me. Ev began by selling those of us who were interested a fiberglass fly rod and a reel spooled with sinking line. The entire class then bought fly tying vises, scissors and the other supplies needed to tie flies. Hooks, thread and other items could be purchased as needed. The supplies needed for the evening's lessons had been laid out ahead of time. We started out tying very simple patterns, the first of which was a Wooly Worm. Ev would demonstrate the technique for tying a fly and then walk around the class assisting as needed while the students, as best they could, duplicated the fly. That first fly I tied was a real looker, but then it's hard to tie anything with mittens on. I'm kidding, of course, but I need some kind of an excuse for how shabby it was. We generally learned three or four patterns at each session. As the weeks passed, the patterns became more complex, and by the last session we were tying some pretty decent looking flies in spite of cold, stiff fingers.

Spring rolled around. I now had a fly rod, reel, some leaders and a box of flies, but I still didn't know how to fly fish, and I had not succeeded in hooking up with anyone to teach me. I had seen guys do fly casting, but I quickly learned that seeing it and doing it were two different things. I couldn't do anything with that fly line, and I had no idea what flies to use for any given situation. On a number of occasions I took a wild, flying guess on the proper fly, flailed the water with errant casts, caught nothing and gave up in frustration. I always went back to that which I had faith in—spinners and worms.

In 1981 I decided to leave the group in Spokane and return to the army. I contacted a friend of mine who was then chief of pathology at the Madigan Army Medical Center. He had an opening and was interested in having me back. I contacted a recruiter in Seattle and negotiated my return. I wanted to return at the same rank I held when I had previously resigned (Lt. Col.), and I wanted all my time in grade reinstated. Lastly, I wanted to be assigned at Madigan. All these requests were granted so once again my family and I returned to Tacoma. This time we did not live in post housing. We bought a house with three acres on the southeast edge of Tacoma not too far from the town of Puyallup. I loved to fish as much as ever, but I was given a very time consuming church calling, and between work, church and three acres of land to maintain, I did not have many evenings or weekends free. My fishing went into something of a hiatus. For vacations we either went to Idaho to visit family or went someplace family oriented like Disneyland. On those occasions when I did fish I used my canoe—until it was stolen from my backyard. I lost my rubber raft to mice and my canoe to thieving rats. I then had no boat at all.

On one of the trips to Idaho to visit my family, I decided that, for old times sake, it would be fun to fish the left hand of Marsh Creek. I invited my youngest sister's son, Scott, then sixteen, to accompany me, and I took my son Randy, who was nine. Randy and I drove to the canyon in my car, and Scott and his best friend, followed on a four wheeler. When we started fishing, the four of us were more or less leap frogging from hole to hole, so we moved rapidly up the canyon. It was a dry year and the creek was very low. Fish were sparse, so we were not catching much, but we were having a good time.

We came upon a small pool within which a large brook trout was trapped. The pool was below a small water fall so the fish could not go upstream, and the water at the lower end was too shallow for the trout to make its way downstream. Scott was fishing with worms, and he dropped his bait into the hole while the other three of us stood back watching. The fish had seen us so it was wary and would not take the bait. After several attempts, Scott set his pole down onto the bank, waded into the pool and scooped the fish out with his hands. It lay flopping on the bank, and Randy started trying to pick it up. He thought catching that fish by hand was the most marvelous thing he had ever witnessed. He was gregarious at all times, but when excited, his mouth ran constantly.

When we decided to return home, we began walking down the canyon, and Randy ran well ahead of us stopping only occasionally to peer into the creek or throw a rock into the water. When we were about a hundred yards from the parking area, we saw a game warden's truck parked next to my car. Randy was animatedly gabbing with the warden. Scott stopped suddenly and sucked in his breath. "You don't suppose Randy will tell the Warden how I caught that fish, do you?" "Oh man," I replied, "I wouldn't be surprised. He has no clue that it was illegal." When we got to our vehicles, the warden greeted us and chatted amiably for a few moments. He then said, "Scott, I hear you caught a pretty nice fish." Scott dropped his gaze to the ground, grinned sheepishly and replied, "Yeh." "How did you catch it?" the warden asked. Yep. Randy blabbed. The warden gave Scott a short lecture and a stern warning and let it go.

During my time in Tacoma, I was asked to be a scout master. I took all the necessary training and learned that, in spite of my participation in scouts as a youth, there was a whole lot about scouting that I did not know and a whole lot of stuff that we did that was not in accordance with scout guidelines. I now did everything by the book, and my boy's summer camps were spent at organized, scout owned camp properties working on merit badges and various crafts. There was, of course, swimming, boating, hiking and other fun stuff. As far as I could tell, the boys had a wonderful time. They always looked forward to it.

We had occasional weekend campouts at places of choice, and for one of those, I decided to take the boys fishing. I won't go so far as to call that decision a dreadful mistake since the boys had fun and, hopefully, learned a little bit but what a lesson in frustration. I became one exasperated scout master. The boys were all 12 and 13 years old and my son, Randy, was the only one that had ever held a fishing pole in his hands. I had never imagined that there could be so many ways to screw up a fishing line. None of the boys had any fishing equipment, so I took along three poles of my own—the one I used and a couple of older ones—and all the poles belonging to my family members. They were all spinning rods and reels. I took the boys to the Potholes Reservoir near Moses Lake Washington. We arrived late Friday evening and found a good place near the lake to set up camp.

The following morning, after a communal breakfast, I showed the boys how to cast, strung up the poles, tied on spinners or various other lures and baited the hooks. As I handed each boy a prepared pole, he set out to find his own place on the bank to fish. By the time I handed the last boy his pole, a small twelve year old polynesian boy returned and presented his pole to me. There was a wad of tangled, monofilament line around the reel the likes of which I had never before seen. I would have thought it impossible to tangle line like that. He had never even succeeded in getting his hook in the water. I set about untangling the mess, but I had barely started when another boy returned with a tangle that was just about as bad. I clenched my jaws to hold my temper and slowly got the bird's nests untangled, their reels and lines back in functional order and their hooks rebaited. I once again went over how to cast and sent them on their way. It was less than five minutes until the polynesian boy was back with another tangle. Once again, I painstakingly untangled the mess and showed him how to cast. Meanwhile, two other boys had returned with tangles or fouled reels and a third boy somehow managed to wrap his leader around a tree branch high above his head and 20 ft. behind him. I was trying to fix those messes when other boys started calling me because they needed more bait. Surprisingly, a couple of boys actually caught fish. Randy was baiting his own hooks and hauling in fish one after another, and he was really lording it over the other boys each time he caught one. He thought he was the hero of the camp. Once again, the Polynesian boy boy returned with a tangle. He was almost as frustrated as I was and said he did not want to fish anymore. I confess. I didn't want him to fish anymore either. I had erroniously thought, when we planned this trip, that I was going to get to fish. Silly me. None of the boys lasted much longer than an hour, and then they were off on the trails along the lake, playing in the water and venturing into the sagebrush desert leaving me with a pile of fishing rods with fouled, tangled, monofilament line. It took me hours to get those spinning reels functional again.

Two boys came running back to say they had encountered a snake on the trail. I went with them and, sure enough, about a hundred yards from our camp, there was a small rattle snake stretched out across the trail. All the boys had gathered to have a look. They wanted to kill it, but I told them to go around it and just leave it alone. Very shortly the snake slithered off into the sagebrush. I told the boys to keep a sharp eye out for snakes and give them a wide berth if they saw any. Under no circumstances were they to get close enough to try to kill one.

At the end of the campout I could summarize the accomplishments of the trip as follows: An overnight sleep out for the boys including experience putting up and taking down tents and preparing sleeping areas; some instruction and experience at camp cooking; a little bit of instruction and experience fishing (very little); recognition of a rattle snake and some instruction regarding encounters; firsthand experience at getting wet and filthy dirty (they were very accomplished at that); recognition by the scout master that he no longer wished to teach 12 or 13 yr. old boys how to fish if there was more than one at a time and to count on absolutely, positively NO fishing for the scout master.

# FLY FISHING FINALLY

In 1989 I retired from the army after a total of 20 years in the armed service. I obtained a position with two other pathologists at the Magic Valley Regional Medical Center, and we moved to Twin Falls, Idaho. Very shortly, I looked up an old friend from my college days, Jim Cox. He was an avid fly fisherman, and it was not long after reuniting with him that my aspiration to fly fishing finally came to pass. If one enjoys fishing, I can think of no finer place to live than Twin Falls, Idaho. Nearby reservoirs, lakes, creeks and rivers abound. Not the least of these is the Snake River. If one wishes to travel some distance, I-34/I-36 with its 80 mph speed limit passes right through the heart of the Magic Valley. World class fisheries such as Henry's Lake are just a few hours away.

By the time we arrived in Twin Falls, it had been about 15 years since I had taken my fly tying classes. I still had my fiberglass rod which I used for a while. It worked fine, of course, but fly rod makers had switched from fiberglass to graphite for their rod stock, and the graphite rods were much lighter, so I figured my equipment must surely be hopelessly out of date. I spent a small fortune getting myself re-outfitted.

Clea and I had lived in Twin Falls no more than a few days when I spied a small, 12 ft., double hull, fiberglass boat with a 15 horse Johnson motor sitting beside a road with a FOR SALE sign. It was on a small trailer. I salivated over it enough that Clea went back and bought it. Do I have a wife or what? I had that boat for about 10 years.

I used the boat frequently, but Jim Cox and Bob Norman were heavily invested in fly fishing from float tubes. I figured if that was what they were doing, it must surely be "the way" to properly fly fish, so I began checking out gear. The Blue Lakes Sporting Goods Store had a package deal. It included a 9 ft., 6 wt. Sage Graphite II fly rod, a Sage reel, fly line, waders, booties, fins and float tube. My birthday was approaching, and once again Clea sprang forward and got me completely outfitted—or so I thought.

As it turned out, during those initial months, every time I went fishing it seemed like I needed something that I didn't have. Jim and

Bob were both excellent fly fishermen, so, naturally, they caught way more fish than I did. Each fishing trip went something like this: I am fishing with a 3 sink line and catching no fish. Jim is catching a lot of fish, so I ask him what line he is using. He replies that he is using a floating line with a sinking tip. Any fly fisherman will tell you that the most important piece of fly fishing equipment is the line, so, naturally, I now have to have floating line with a sinking tip. When we return home I go to Blue Lakes Sporting Goods at my earliest opportunity, buy a new spool for my reel, and have them put on a floating line with sinking tip with appropriate backing. This scene played out over and over until before long I had spools of 1 sink, 2 sink, 3 sink, 4 sink, floating line, floating line with sinking tip, and, eventually, intermediate sink line. Now, many years later, most of those lines ride around in my bag of gear.

The same situation applied to flies. I had not tied flies for many years. I had a vise and other equipment, but some of those 15 year old feathers were in sorry shape. I purchased hooks, fur and feathers and began tying up patterns I had learned in class. Unfortunately, nobody was much using those patterns anymore, so I bought books on fly tying and began to catch up.

Once again, when I went fishing Jim and Bob were often hauling fish in while I was getting nothing. I now had the same line on that they did so I ask what flies they are using. Always, it was something that I didn't have, and, furthermore, did not have the proper fur or feathers to tie. Back to the fly shop. I then tied up a good supply of that pattern but on the next trip it was something else. I eventually tied dozens of patterns all of which will catch fish but few of which, in recent years, get used. It also took me a long time to learn to tie sturdy flies that do not come apart after catching two or three fish. The flies I tie these days would never be called works of art, but they rarely come apart, and I often can catch forty or fifty fish before the fly wears out. The interesting thing is, the fish frequently don't care whether or not the fly is worn. I've had flies that the hackle was ripped off and the body was worn down to just a hook shank wrapped with lead. The fly still had a tail, though, and it was still catching fish. At other times, the fish can be really picky. You never know.

Clea and I bought a home which is near Rock Creek Canyon. The canyon is a wonderful place teeming with wildlife including a resident deer herd that occasionally comes out of the canyon and wanders into the backyards of my neighbors and myself. I can leave the house and be down the canyon fishing in ten to fifteen minutes—or at least I could before arthritis and total knee replacements took their tole.

Fortunately, I no longer have a desire to fish Rock Creek. Up until ten years ago, the fishing was excellent. There is a fish hatchery on the opposite side of the canyon, and until the new owners did some remodeling quite a few fish apparently escaped into the creek—and probably some fish pellets to boot. In any case, the fishing from the hatchery for about a mile downstream was fantastic, and the best part was, not many people knew it. I had been fly fishing only a short while the first time I made the 100 ft. climb down the canyon wall with my chest waders and wading boots on. I was a little sweaty doing it that way, but it was impractical to carry the waders and boots down the canyon, put them on there, and then have to retrace your steps after you've fished a half mile up or down stream to retrieve your regular shoes to climb back up. I wondered about that at times, though, after making the climb in those waders on a warm day.

I had done a lot of creek fishing in my boyhood days but never with a fly. On my first trip to the creek, I arrived at the bottom of the canyon, took a moment to wipe the sweat off my forehead and waded into the stream across from a deep hole where the fast moving water crashed into a curve in the bank and created a large eddie. Completely focused on the hole, I paid no attention to what was behind me. I made my first false cast, started my second and—aw, shit! My fly had taken about six turns around a Russian Olive branch. There was no getting it down, so I broke it off and tied on a new leader and fly. I moved a bit toward the middle of the stream so my backcasts were up stream and managed to drop the fly just above the hole.

It had barely touched the water when an eighteen inch rainbow shot out of the hole and grabbed it. It made a few frantic tugs and then darted into the current. It used the current to race downstream, but it was well hooked, and I managed to turn it. I worked it into slow moving water and finally got it into my net. I caught two more fish from that hole and then began wading downstream, fishing ahead of me. Russian Olive branches overhung the creek almost everywhere making regular casting almost impossible, so I had to learn to roll cast. Even then, over the years, I left those trees well festooned with leader and flies. I could sometimes catch 15 or 20 fish with occasional ones over eighteen inches in three or four hours. Then the fish hatchery was sold, and the new owners put an end to escaping fish. In that same time frame, Idaho Power built a small dam across the mouth of the creek to generate electricity, so fish could no longer run up Rock Creek from the Snake River. Since that time, the fishing has been poor and I no longer bother to go down the canyon.

Before I discovered Rock Creek, and shortly after I acquired my float tube, Jim Cox took me to a small reservoir a few miles south of Jackpot, Nevada. We kicked out onto the water, and Jim showed me how to cast, count the fly down and retrieve. We had not gone far when I realized I had left my fly box at the truck. The only fly I had with me was on the end of my line. I turned around and started kicking back to the boat ramp dragging the fly behind me. Suddenly a 20 inch German brown stuck. It ripped some line off my reel then turned toward me. I cranked furiously trying to keep the slack out of my line. The fish turned again and, once more, started ripping out line. I was having the time of my life. It was the most fun I had ever had catching a fish. You might say the fish was hooked—but so was I!

# ROSEWORTH RESERVOIR

I parked my pick-up on the drying mud of the west bank of the reservoir and set my float tube next to the water. I strung up my new Sage rod, donned my waders and the rest of my gear and stepped into my tube. I picked the tube up and backed into the water. It was only two feet deep near the shore, so I had to back out several feet before I could set the tube on the water and settle into the saddle. I kicked out about thirty feet and cast back toward the shore. I made only a few strips when my line stopped dead. I thought I had snagged a weed. I gave my line a good tug, and that weed took off. A nice rainbow exploded out of the water, circled me running toward deeper water and then leapt again. When I finally played it into the net, I was pleased to find a nice 16 inch fish.

The Roseworth Reservoir (also known as Cedar Creek Reservoir) is a small impoundment less that an hour's drive south of Twin Falls. It is on a sagebrush prairie about 15 miles beyond the Salmon Dam Reservoir. It is fed, mostly, by two large creeks entering the upper end, but there is a large spring which runs into the lower end. Because of its accessability, the lower end is a popular place for bait fishermen to cast from the shore, and a green, grassy area near the spring is a popular place for camping. Fish and Game keeps the reservoir well stocked with rainbow trout, and, ordinarily, there are fish ranging from fingerlings to nice, fat fish 13 to 15 inches. These planters are often rapidly removed by bank fishermen and trollers, but there is always some carry-over and occasionally conditions are right so that a whole class of fish survives to become considerably larger. When one gets into those fish he can often do very well. It is almost as if every fish came from the same mold.

The year I acquired my float tube the reservoir held a large population of trout which were about 16 inches, fat as footballs and very strong. I became aware of the reservoir, as I did most of the fisheries in the area, through Jim Cox, and I started going there frequently. Initially, I was familiar with the lower end, so that was where I usually put my tube into the water. Fish were attracted to that area because of the cold spring, an abundance of weeds and willows which provided cover and numerous aquatic insects. My casting was pretty rough, but I could manage to get my fly into the water and drag it behind me. I had not yet grasped the concept of catch and release, so I thought a great day of fishing was when I caught my limit. The limit at Roseworth was (and is) six fish, and I could usually manage to limit out in five or six hours. I thought I was really becoming a first class fly fisherman. I would rush home, call Jim, and extoll the wonderful fishing. "I caught my limit," I would exclaim. "Well that's great," Jim would invariably reply giving no hint of his undoubted amusement. My ego deflated rapidly, when I was with Jim or Bob Norman, whether on Roseworth or any other reservoir, and I saw that they caught way more than six fish. I yet had much to learn. I soon recognized that I was pretty much putting my fly in the water, just kicking around and trolling.

Jim and Robert both spoke of catching very large fish in Roseworth, but almost everything I caught was those 16 inch fish or smaller catchables. Jim and I occasionally fished farther up the reservoir, but I was convinced the best fishing was on the lower end, so that was where I plopped my tube when I went there by myself.

One evening I drove to Roseworth fully intending to fish. I pulled in on the lower end of the lake, as usual, and I spotted a pick-up camper near the water's edge. I pulled alongside and exchanged a few pleasantries with the two women who owned it. I viewed the shoreline ahead of the camper. This was nearer the water than I had thought I could go, and it looked pretty muddy, but the ground under the camper had the same appearance and it seemed to be solid, so I pulled onward thinking to move forward another hundred feet or so before putting my tube in the water.

At that time, I had a 1992 Ford 250 pick-up with four wheel drive. In order for the front wheel drive to work, you had to get out and lock the wheel hubs. I had not driven more than 30 ft. when my pick-up sank in mud almost to the axles. I immediately put the shift lever into four wheel drive and tried to back out. No dice. I tried rocking it, but that didn't work. I had some six foot planks in the back of the truck that I carried with me to level my 5th wheel. I borrowed a shovel from the women and began digging. I dug a trench behind each wheel and laid a plank into it. I got back into the truck and tried to move backward. Still no deal. I got out and dug some more. Finally, after about two hours of sweating and silently cursing, the wheels gripped the planks, and I backed onto solid ground. As I was loading the muddy planks it suddenly struck me; I forgot to lock the wheel hubs. I had moved the shift lever but without locking the hubs I did the whole operation with only rear wheel drive. Perhaps had I been in four wheel drive I could have driven out of the mess without all the digging. Anyway, I was a muddy mess, and it was too late to fish so I drove home very thoroughly ticked off at myself.

During the spring of the year 2000, Clea and I attended a boat show at the Filer, Idaho fairgrounds. I spotted a 16 ft. Crestliner with a 40 horse motor, and I said to Clea, "Man, that is my idea of a fishing boat. I've always wanted one like that." She said, "Well, if you want it, buy it"—so I did.

Shortly thereafter, Jim and I went to Roseworth to fish. By then I had been fly fishing for ten years and had become a devoted advocate of catch and release, but the water in Roseworth is cold and clean in the springtime, and trout caught from there are usually very good to eat, so on this day I decided I wanted to keep three fish. I soon realized that keeping any fish was going to be a problem. The fishing was terrible. We fished for several hours and caught nothing.

At Jim's suggestion, I headed the boat toward the upper end, and we began parking, at intervals, over the old creek channel. Finally, I hooked a nice 14 inch fish. I brought it to the boat and, without thinking, reached over the side and flipped the hook out of its lip. I had barely done so when I said, "Oh shoot! I wanted to keep some fish." Suddenly, the fish came floating to the surface belly up. This seemed strange as the fish had not been badly hooked, had seemed uninjured and was certainly not exhaused when I released it. I laughed and said, "Who says fishermen's prayers are not answered." I reached out with the net, scooped up the fish and dropped it into the live bait well. A short while later, Jim hooked a fish. He got it about half way to the boat when it threw the hook. A few moments later it, too, popped to the surface. I scooped it into the net and dropped it into the well.

Jim and I were laughing ourselves silly over this turn of events but were basically scratching our heads for an explanation. I hooked another fish. It was not very big, so when I got it alongside the boat I tried to lift it over the side instead of using the net. It came off the hook, dropped back into the water and swam away. It quickly disappeared from sight, but suddenly, several feet from the boat, it popped to the surface belly up. I moved the boat within reach, and I scooped it into the net just as it was flipping over to swim away. I had my three fish and, strangely, we never had so much as another strike. I remain baffled to this day. There were no other dead fish on the water so toxins or low oxygen concentrations would not seem to be a consideration. The fish had appeared healthy and uninjured when hooked and fighting. Moreover, they were alive and healthy in the live bait well hours later when I arrived home with my boat. I have no explanation for what I experienced that day. As expected, though, the fish were really good to eat.

It is common knowledge that fishing is sometimes very good just before a thunderstorm. The experts say that if a storm is close enough to hear the thunder there is potential for a lightening strike, and one should seek shelter. Even knowing this, if you are really catching fish, it is hard to get off the water when a storm seems to be off in a distance. On day Jim Cox and I were fishing Roseworth in float tubes, and a thunderstorm was forming many miles off to the south. We could barely hear the thunder and were essentially paying it no attention until I made a cast and called out, "Hey, Jim. When I made that last cast I got a spark of static electricity between my index finger and my pole." "Really!" He exclaimed. "I guess it's time for us to get off the water. It's not a great idea to be waving a graphite lightening rod around in a thunder storm." The storm still appeared to be several miles away, and I was surprised that the air around us was so electrically charged. We kicked to shore, climbed out of the water, layed our rods flat on the ground and prepared to wait out the storm. We did not have long to wait. Within a few minutes we could see ripples on the water as a fast moving wind approached, and then we were blasted with a 30 mph gust. We were glad to be off the water. Moments later, the rain started, and we were pelted with a downpour of huge raindrops and small hail stones. Since we had chest waders on, we did not get wet, but the cold rain blasting into our faces was uncomfortable. Jim had a raincoat, so we huddled together and put his coat over our heads. Within a half hour, the storm had passed to the north, and the rain had stopped. We returned to the water and resumed our fishing, but I learned that day to have a great deal of respect for thunderstorms. I feel guilty sometimes when storms are approaching because I think there are times when we are in my boat that I clear off the water before I really need to and maybe cheat my partner out of some fishing time, but I've witnessed a lot of thunderstorms over the ensuing years and I'd just as soon live to witness a few more.

One evening, Jim Sorenson and I launched my boat at the ramp half way down the reservoir and ran straight across to the other side. The water near the far shore was shallow but dropped off rather quickly. Fish often hold on that drop-off. I tossed my anchor in 12 ft. of water and we began to fish. We were doing quite well but had not fished long when a mild breeze began to blow. We decided to run down the reservoir and use the breeze to drift back along the shoreline. That turned out to be excellent idea because the fishing went from pretty good to very good.

With each cast, I stripped in my line and dropped it onto the bottom of the boat, a standard fly fishing technique. At the end of the third drift, I stripped in my line, dropped it onto the bottom of the boat and set my pole down with the tip protruding beyond the stern. I did not notice that my fly had dropped into the water. I turned the boat to run up wind for another drift and shoved the throttle forward. Apparently, my fly was dragging in the water and the sudden accelleration ripped out the line from the bottom of the boat. In my peripheral vision I saw my $300 fly rod lift into the air, and I heard a loud "thunk" as my reel hit the stern. I yanked the throttle back hoping the reel had snagged up on the stern but no such luck. I turned in time to see my fly rod sinking out of sight. I spun the boat around and returned to the place I thought I had last seen it, but it was impossible to know the exact spot. Jim and I drug the anchor on the bottom hoping to snag the flyline. I strung up my spare rod, and he and I made long casts, letting our flies drop to the bottom, and we drug them back hoping to snag either the pole or the fly line. Nothing worked and I was disraught. All we managed to snag was a few weeds and rocks.

In late September and early October when the reservoir water was low I returned several times, parked the boat and walked the bottom hoping to find my fly rod down in the mud. No such luck. I did, however, find a very nice spinning rod and reel which had been lost, apparently, in much the same manner as I lost my fly rod. It cleaned up well, and I gave it to one of my grandkids. I recovered two other spinning rods from Henry's Lake over the years because my fly snagged either the pole or the line, and I dragged them up from the bottom, so this kind of loss is apparently not an unusual occurrence. You can only recover them, it seems, when it isn't yours and you are not really trying.

The year following the loss of my pole an event happened that changed forever my approach to fishing Roseworth. Since there are many places to fish in this part of Idaho I had never fished Roseworth in the early spring, and by mid-July the water has usually been drawn down enough to preclude getting into the extreme upper end. One beautiful, spring day in early June, I went fishing alone, and I launched my boat at the upper boat ramp and headed up the reservoir. It was late enough in the season that the muddy spring run-off had cleared but early enough that the reservoir was still nearly full. I stopped and anchored at several promising places but had no luck. I considered heading back down the reservoir but decided instead to do a little exploring. As I proceeded into the inlet, the water began to get pretty shallow, so I pulled back the throttle and idled slowly forward. Soon the water was six feet deep, and weeds were sticking above the surface.

I again considered turning back down the reservoir, but I looked over near the shore and observed a lone fly fisherman in a tube about 200 feet from me, and he was catching fish. He was doing his best to remain inconspicuous, but it was hard to do when he had a fish on nearly all the time. I threw out my anchor and made a cast. The fly had barely hit the water when a fish grabbed it. For two hours I caught a fish almost every cast. Many of them were ten inch catchables but there were also many fish up to fifteen inches, and a few that were even larger. It was wonderful!

I finally had to go home, but I could hardly wait to come back, so two days later, I returned to the same spot. The fish were still there, and I again had an extraordinary day. After that outing, in spite of my eagerness, it was two weeks before I had another chance to fish. I returned to that same spot, but the water had dropped two feet and the fish were gone.

The next spring, the latter part of May, Jim Cox and I launched into Roseworth with his boat which is somewhat smaller than mine, and we proceeded up the reservoir into water less than two feet deep. We maneuvered ourselves over the creekbed between the willows. The water was about six feet deep in the channel. We threw his anchor into a willow to keep the creek from pushing us downstream and began to fish. I had heard that there were large fish in Roseworth, but this was the day I became a believer. We not only found big fish, there were a lot of them. It was astounding. Apparently the big guys like the shallow, cold, crystal clear water in and near the creek. Jim and I now try to get out to Roseworth in the early spring as soon as the muddy water has cleared. On really good water years, we can get up into those willows until early July but mid-June is more common.

One day in early July, Jim and I were sitting fishing and watching Damsel nymphs crawing up the base of the willows. Trout could be seen making small dimples in the water as they picked those nymphs off the weeds. Two large Dragon flies in a conjugal embrace came fluttering in front of our faces. Suddenly, there was an explosion out of the willows, and an orange breasted black bird snatched the dragon fly pair in mid-air. He was so close I could have whacked him with my fly rod. He nearly startled Jim and me out of the boat. That bird got enough food in one grab to last him all day. He flew a few moments until he had swallowed the bugs and then returned to his original spot in the willows, paying absolutely no attention to two old fogies in an aluminum boat. Once we became aware of them, numerous birds were seen nearby working their way along the base of the willows nabbing damsel nymphs. Once the water drops and one can no longer get up into the willows the fishing is often good farther down the reservoir, but catching one of those big guys is rare.

# IN SEARCH OF THE BIG ONE

Robert Norman and Jim Cox are superb fishermen. Robert got to be more or less bored with catching small fish a long time ago, so he and Jim always had their antennae tuned for stories of places where big fish abound. I was always happy when I got to tag along whether the fish were big or small. One evening at a Magic Valley Fly Fishers Meeting somebody brought in an ad from the internet for a place near Cody, Wyoming called "MONSTER LAKE" touting trout averaging eight pounds. It was a pay to fish place, and it was expensive, but Jim said to me, "Do you want to go?" and we soon had reservations for a couple of days the latter part of May.

Our route took us through Yellowstone Park, so getting there was half the fun. We had plenty of time to dawdle, so, on a whim, we stopped and fished the upper end of Island Park Reservoir for a couple of hours. I didn't accomplish much more than getting my float tube wet. We then entered Yellowstone National Park through the west gate and thoroughly enjoyed a leisure trip across the park on the way to the east gate, where we exited. Buffalo, Elk and other game abounded, and every river we passed left us wishing we had the time and the means to fish them all, and it spiked our anticipation for the touted hugh fish awaiting us at Monster Lake. Wild animals have no knowledge of park boundaries, so the ride from the east gate down to Cody is almost as interesting as the park itself. That was the only stretch of highway I have ever been on where we had to stop to let big horn sheep cross the road. It was just after sundown as we approached Cody, and there were huge herds of deer on the ranch hay fields. I wondered how those ranchers salvaged anything for their cattle.

It was late evening when we checked in at Monster Lake, and our rooms were superb. After traveling all day we were tired, so we went to bed early, and we slept soundly in spite of adrenalin caused by dreams of hauling in big fish. We arose early, ate a cold breakfast from our coolers and were on the lake in our float tubes at the crack of dawn. It did not take long to start catching fish. It also did not take long to realize that the touted eight pound average was a gross exaggeration. In fact, a stated four pound average would have been an exaggeration, though perhaps just a mild one. Never-the-less, we caught a lot of fish most of which were 18 to 20 inches, and they were strong and feisty. We continued to fish throughout the day in spite of a stiff wind that arose around noon—a constant phenomenon in Wyoming, we learned.

On our second day we arose to find that the wind was still blowing, and it had intensified considerably—not a good day for tubing. We went to the end of the lake, with the wind to our backs, and began casting from the shore. Jim and Robert were hooking a lot of fish and were happy fishing that way. I could not seem to cast quite far enough, so I decided that wind or no wind, I was going to go out on the water in my tube. Once on the water I turned my back to the wind, so I was generally kicking towards the bank, but I was gradually losing ground. I was catching fish, though, so I was satisfied to let the wind push me whereever it pleased.

After a few hours I realized that my bladder was full, and I was going to have to do something about it. I was less than pleased to further realize that I was now in the middle of the lake. As I pondered the situation, I figured I could probably kick back to shore in about an hour. My bladder situation was uncomfortable, but I was sure I could last that long. I cast out my line and began vigorously kicking toward the shore, dragging my fly behind me. It was tough going into that wind, and just as I was convinced that I was making some headway a fish grabbed my fly. By the time I got it into the net and unhooked it I had lost all the progress I had made and probably a little more. I started out again, but the same thing happened. I considered letting the wind blow me the rest of the way across the lake, but at some point I was going to have to make my way back, and I did not relish the idea of kicking across the entire lake into that wind. I decided that the best thing to do was to kick into the wind as I had before, but to not let myself get distracted if I hooked a fish. I set out once more. Once again, just as I was making good progress, a fish slammed my fly. I tried to concentrate on keeping my back to the wind and keeping those fins moving, but that fish was strong. It turned me first one way and then the other, and every time it turned me I lost headway. When turned sidewise to the wind the tube would move over my legs so that my kicks became ineffective. I struggled to get straightened out and keep kicking, but I wasn't going anywhere.

Finally, after several attempts, I gave up the fishing, reeled in my line and put my full effort into kicking to shore. I had lost considerable time with my aborted attempts, and I was still at least an hour out. I did not want to give up an hour of fishing time, but I was truly desperate. By the time I reached shore, I was one anxious dude, and as soon as my feet touched ground the old "I'm gonna get to pee soon" anticipation kicked in causing bladder spasms and making the stress all the worse. I thought for sure that after all that effort to get to shore I was going to wet myself before I could get my waders off. Somehow, through what I can only describe as super human effort, I averted disaster. I was too tired to go out in the tube again, so I spent the afternoon fishing from the bank.

A year later the quest for big fish once again beckoned. Jim heard of another pay to fish facility near Evanston Wyoming on the Guild family ranch. He had heard that the fishing was so good that Denny Rickards (well known fly fisherman and author) held a fly fishing clinic there every June. It seems the present ranch owner's father had grown old and infirmed and was no longer able to do ranch work, so his sons stocked a few fish in their irrigation reservoir, so the old man would have a place to fish. To their surprise and delight, it was not long until the old man was bringing in some spectacular fish, and the boys realized they were on to something. The middle of May, Robert, Jim and I set out for Evanston. The Guild family members turned out to be wonderful people, but we learned that the fishing did not really turn on until early June. After coming that far we decided to try our luck anyway, and for us it turned out to be O.K. but not spectacular.

We started fishing at the crack of dawn on the upper end of the reservoir. We had been fishing for about an hour when my pole was almost ripped out of my hands. My slack line was quickly stripped through the guides, and my reel started to spin. Line was disappearing at an incredible rate, and I half way expected the reel to start smoking. I was soon well into my backing, and line was still going out. My adrenalin surged, and I was convinced that I had hooked my biggest fish ever. I yelled to Jim that I had hooked a monster. I was having a glorious time! The fish did not jump, and it did not deviate left nor right. It did not circle my tube nor come back toward me. It just kept going straight ahead with incredible strength. Finally, it eased up a bit and I began to reel it in, but every time I made a little headway, it took off again—always straight away from me. I cranked on that reel until my arms ached, but I was gradually winning the battle. Finally I got it close enough to get a glimpse of my trophy fish. Aw man, what a disappointment. It was a nice fish, maybe about 18 or 19 inches, but it was no monster. It had pulled so hard and ran so straight because I had foul hooked it in the tail.

Jim, Robert and I spread out over the reservoir. About 9 AM I ended up in a small bay fed by a small stream coming from a spring a few yards away. I had not been catching much, so I started playing with different fly patterns. I tied on a fly that Marv Taylor calls a Taylor shrimp except that I tied it with yellow and black variegated chenille instead of dark olive and gold. The fish went crazy. For the next hour, I caught really nice fish. Jim was fishing about fifteen minutes away from me, so I kicked over to him and, with great excitement, informed him of the great fishing I had blundered into. I lead him back with great expectations and—nothing. I don't know if the fish had moved or if they had quit biting, but my ego and my credibility took a devastating hit. Sometimes I wonder why I like fishing. By then it was about noon, and the expected wind came whooping down the canyon and across the reservoir. It never did get strong enough to stop us from fishing, but it made tubing very difficult and wore us out. Robert was fishing in a somewhat sheltered area near the dam and was doing quite well. Jim and I joined him. Jim caught a few fish, but not as many as Robert. Old Carl never touched a fish the rest of the afternoon.

As an aside, I took my son-in-law to the Guild ranch a year later in early July. I was hoping to hit the tail end of that touted June turn-on. The reservoir was buried under fishermen from Ogden. A group of six of them had walkie talkies to keep in touch, and they were spread all over the lake. I had expected wind at noon, but it was only 10 AM when it came whooping down the reservoir, and it was followed by a thunderstorm. I expected it would quickly pass, but it stayed right over the reservoir. Thunder cracked and lightning popped all afternoon. Hyrum and I fished for two hours in the morning and spent the rest of the day sitting in the truck. We never touched a fish. The only good news was that the Guild brothers cut the price to fish in half.

Jim, Robert and I spent the night in Evanston and arose early the next morning and headed west on Interstate 80. Instead of turning toward Ogden onto Interstate 84 we stayed on 80 heading toward Salt Lake City and then turned onto highway 40 and drove to Heber City, Utah. We found a sporting goods store where we purchased Utah fishing licenses and then continued on highway 40 up Daniel's Pass to Strawberry Reservoir. We threw our tubes into the water at a place called The Ladders and fished for a couple of hours without catching anything. We ate some sandwiches and drove around the reservoir to a small bay where Mud Creek runs in. Robert's hope was to get into some large rainbows.

We launched our tubes and kicked to the far side of the narrow bay without catching anything. We then kicked deeper into the bay, and the water became increasingly shallow. When we reached 9 foot water I changed from a 3 sink to a 2 sink line and tied a hare's ear pattern on the dropper and a Psychedelic P Quad on the end. On my first cast, I nailed a nineteen inch cutthroat on the P Quad. I caught fish regularly the rest of the afternoon on both flies. As usual, though, my catch rate was substantially less than Robert's. It seemed like every time I looked in his direction, he had his pole in the air playing a fish.

As the afternoon wore on, Robert became aware of a twentyish young man wearing a cowboy hat who was following him. He was catching nothing. Finally, he called to Robert, "Hey man, what line and what fly are you using?" Robert told him what line to use and told him to use small nymphs. The young man restrung his fly rod and then called out, "Hey man, let me see your fly." Robert stripped in his line and showed the youngster the two flies he had on. The kid's face fell and he said, "Oh man, I don't have nothin' like that." Robert gave him two flies. The young man tied on one of the flies and continued to closely follow Robert. Robert continued to catch fish, and the young man continued to catch nothing. It was like that the rest of the afternoon. Finally, we quit fishing and began packing our gear. Jim was laughing about the young man's ineptitude and frustration. We had all been stripping the flies through the water rather rapidly. The young dude with the cowboy hat had been very slowly working his fly. Jim asked Robert, "Why didn't you tell him to strip fast?" Robert replied, "I told him what line to use. I showed him the flies to use and even gave him a couple. I told him how to count the fly down, and he was following me like I had him on a leash. After all of that, if he is too dumb to watch what kind of strip I'm doing, he doesn't deserve to catch fish."

The Strawberry Reservoir is an easy drive from Lehi, Utah, which is where my daughter and her husband lived for several years. After this experience with Jim and Robert, I made it a point to visit my daughter and take my son-in-law fishing, and we made a trip to Strawberry just a short time later. My son-in-law had never fly fished until I took him, and we had enjoyed a couple of previous outings at Roseworth and Magic Reservoirs catching trout and a few perch.

On this afternoon, we set out in our tubes in the bay near Mud Creek, and I had great expectations of catching nice trout. To my dismay, the bay was full of chubs. The reservoir is stocked with cutthroat and rainbow trout. It is supposed to be the cutthroat's job to feast on chubs. It appeared they were not doing their job. The one cutthroat I did catch spit out a 10 inch rainbow. I learned to fish catching chubs and I've caught many dozens of them over the years, but these were the biggest chubs I'd ever seen. Some of them were fourteen and fifteen inches. I've never before or since seen chubs biting so avidly. We were catching big chubs one after another, and, since I was fishing with two flies, I often had two on at a time. After a while I approached Hyrum rather apologetically and said, "I'm sorry, Hy. I thought we'd catch trout, but we're into all these chubs. If you want, we can pack up and try somewhere else." He gave me an incredulous look and said, "Man, what are you apologizing for? This is the most fish I ever caught in my life, and I don't care if they are chubs."

Going after the big fish does not always mean fishing for trout. One evening Jim, Robert and I were fishing the Walcott Reservoir near Rupert, Idaho. There was a small bay off one side of the lake, and large schools of carp were surfacing. We moved into the bay and began casting. Those carp would slurp up whatever Robert or Jim threw out. I caught two of them right away and then could not get another. I had foul hooked carp on previous occasions, but that was the first time I ever got one to take a fly. Carp are considered by most to be a trash fish, but they are relatively hard to catch and a big one can really give you a good pull. If you don't plan on eating the fish, and, for the most part, you catch and release, who cares what the species is?

On another occasion, Jim, Robert and I were fishing the Brownlee Reservoir on the Idaho/Oregon border. Robert thought he had snagged a log, but when the log began to move he realized that he had a fish of some sort, and whatever it was, it was big. When he finally worked it to the net, he found he had hooked a very large flat head catfish.

ROBERT NORMAN WITH FLATHEAD CATFISH
CAUGHT IN BROWNLEE RESERVOIR

As evening approached we encountered a situation much like we had found with the carp at Walcott. There was a large area of shallow water, and catfish were rising. We caught several of them casting flies. None were as big as the flathead cat, but they were all large fish. Until that day I was ignorant of the fact that catfish could be caught with a fly. It really does not happen often—unless your name is Robert.

If you live in Eastern or South Eastern Idaho there is really no need to travel to far places to catch big fish. When one takes such trips it more about the adventure of the trip, being with your fishing buddies and the excitement of fishing somewhere new and different than it is about fish size. It would be hard to find bigger trout than those in the

Snake River or one of its many reservoirs. The biggest trout I ever caught was out of the American Falls Reservoir just above the dam. It was during the summer doldrums, and the fish was deep into cooler water. Like many extremely large fish it didn't have much fight in it, but it was heavy and not a bit interested in being hauled up into warmer water. It was like hauling in a log. That baby was big, though, and it certainly had not been deprived of groceries. My hooking that big fish was more or less serendipity. The American Falls reservoir is very large, and to be consistenly successful one must invest the time to learn the reservoir well—something I have not done.

The Portneuf river arises on the Ft. Hall Indian Reservation and feeds the Chesterfield Reservoir. It flows 124 miles and enters the Snake River near the upper end of the American Falls Reservoir (again on ShoBan property) about ten miles from the city of Pocatello. Very large fish migrate out of American Falls water into the Snake River and then into the Portneuf. Those possessing reservation fishing licenses and who know the river can catch those lunkers. My high school friend, Delene Covert, married a man who has fished the Portneuf for many years, and continues to do so. Considering what he pulls out of there, why go anywhere else?

GEORGE COVERT WITH RAINBOW CAUGHT
IN PORTNEUF RIVER ABOVE AMERICAN FALLS

Over the years I have caught many varieties of fish on a fly. I have caught rainbow trout, cutthroat trout, German brown trout, brook trout, whitefish, kokanee, walleye, bass (both large and small mouth), crappie, blue gill, yellow perch, suckers, pikes minnows (squaw fish), chubs, carp and cat fish, all on a fly. Some fish are large by anybody's standards. Others are large for the variety of fish it is. A thirteen inch blue gill is a very large fish—for a blue gill. I've never hooked a fish that was not fun to catch. Little ones don't count for much but there is some satisfaction in knowing that you got them to take your fly. Basically, they are better than catching nothing.

# SHIP ISLAND LAKE

The hot July sun beat down on the large, goose-neck horse trailer, and a thick cloud of dust roiled from the pick-up as it sped along the gravel road at 40 mph. The horses and mules inside the trailer were becoming restless from the heat and the dirt. After 60 miles on the gravel road, they were coated with fine dry dust, and there were rings of mud around their nostrils. Ken slowed when he spotted the turn-off to the Big Horn Crags campground. Finally, there were just 15 more miles to endure before we reached the trailhead—15 miles on a sorry excuse for what was called an unimproved road. It was indeed unimproved. It was steep, rutted, partially washed out in places, and there were protruding boulders. There were also sharp, hairpin curves that were difficult to negotiate with a trailer. It took over an hour to cover those last 15 miles. I did not see how anyone could even consider traveling that road in a sedan, but there were those who did.

My association with Ken Hulse began about three years earlier when he and his wife, Pat, contracted to do the billing for our pathology group.

Ken Hulse is one of this world's most pleasant individuals. He stands about six feet tall and, at the time we met, his dark hair was turning grey. The corners of his mouth turn upward so that he seems to be perpetually smiling, and, back then, he had a lot to be smiling about as he had what I regarded as the world's best job. I teased him that Pat did all the work, and he did all the playing. In truth, Ken worked very hard, but on superficial examination it looked like play because he very much loved what he was doing. Ken was the office's computer guru, and anytime there was a computer malfunction or a change in the billing process Ken was the fixer upper, and on those occasions he spent long hours in the office. When he was not so occupied he ran his small ranch and that's where his heart was.

He had several head of saddle horses, a few mules and several acres of pasture and hay. I do not know the commercial aspects of his operation as I never asked. He loved horses and spent many hours every week riding, and he frequently assisted a rancher friend from Rogerson, Idaho on cattle drives and other cattle related operations.

One day Ken was in my office and he mentioned that he and a friend had just returned from a horse packing trip to Ship Island Lake. I was suddenly on full alert. Unknown to him, Ship Island Lake was one of my favorite places. I had been there twice previously—once as a boy scout and once as a boy scout chaperone, and I could not and would not pass up an opportunity to go there again.

Back in the days of my youth belonging to our boy scout troop was almost a rite of passage. It was not until many years later when I became a scout master that I realized that there was a lot of stuff we did back then that was not really done the boy scout way. We did spend some time working on merit badges and rank advancement, but I know of only three boys who went on BSA jamborees in the summer and none of us ever went to an official scout camp. I know of only two brothers who obtained the rank of Eagle Scout, and it was laughingly said that it was their mother who earned it. All of us boys carried hunting knives when we went camping and some of the older boys and scout masters even carried side arms. Carrying knives other than small folding pocket knives, at the time I became a scout master, was absolutely forbidden, but I suppose a lot of that difference had to do with our rural way of life and changing times. When I was in high school we often had our deer rifles in our cars during deer season, and if we were going hunting after school we often carried our hunting knives on our belt throughout the school day. Nobody thought anything about it, and nobody every shot up the school.

While we may have done much wrong regarding scouting, there was much we did right. Our scout masters were mostly ranchers and farmers. They loved the boys and devoted much time to scouting activities. We were taught to be hard working, honorable people. The Boy Scout code was taken very seriously. In the summers they took us on frequent overnight campouts into the surrounding canyons, and in July or August there was always one five or six day camping trip usually into the Idaho primitive area. Once again things then were done considerably different than would be tolerated now. There were no seatbelts in those days, and we boys were transported in the backs of open pick-up trucks. I was very small for my age and on one trip the bigger boys picked me up by my legs and dangled me over the back end of the pick-up with my head just inches from the pavement. They expected me to be terrified, but, in that, they were disappointed. The highway moving below me at 60 mph was somewhat disconcerting, but I was confident that they would not purposely drop me so I simply hung there perfectly still, so there was no chance that I would accidently slip from their grasp. Horseplay such as that was, of course, not tolerated by the scout masters when they saw it. We were taught a lot about respect for nature and how to survive in the wilderness. My first such campout was at age 12 and my last at age 16. There were, altogether, five of those fine adventures and one of those trips was to Ship Island Lake.

Ship Island Lake is located at 7400 ft. above sea level in the Frank Church Wilderness Area. In the mid-1990s it was accessed from the Big Horn Crags trail head which is at 9000 ft. elevation in the Yellow Jacket Mountains. The trail head is about 40 miles from Challis, Idaho as the crow flies but is considerably longer by road.

When Ken understood my passion for Ship Island he asked if I would like to make a trip there with him, and the following July Ken and I made the first of four trips. After the first one we both agreed that this was something we needed to do every summer as long as we were able. The trips with Ken were considerably different than my scout experiences. In those youthful days the scout masters had a couple of pack horses that they used to transport their own stuff including their fishing gear, a rubber raft and a small gas motor. We boys carried our gear on our backs. Traveling into the wilderness with Ken was like moving with a first class outfitter. We both rode saddle horses and used mules and pack horses to carry our gear. On that first trip Ken brought only two mules for packing, and we slept on the ground in a small tent. On all future trips he brought a third pack horse, and we slept on cots in a big wall tent. He also packed a small propane stove, a shower bag and an ice chest filled with dry ice to keep our steaks frozen. It was deluxe camping, and we ate well!

I finished my rotating internship at the Tripler Army Medical Center (TAMC) near Honolulu the end of June, 1965. I had two weeks of leave plus travel time before beginning my pathology residency at the Madigan Army Medical Center in Tacoma Washington, so I went home to Downey, Idaho. The first Sunday I was home, I went to church with my parents, and there I was approached by Roy Larsen, a man I had known my whole life. He told me he was leaving the next day to take a troop of explorer scouts to Ship Island Lake. Would I, he asked, like to go along since he really did need a second adult leader? I couldn't believe my good fortune. I went home and dug out all of my old scout camping gear including the most worthless sleeping bag on the planet. Realizing that I was now a doctor, I packed an unusually large first aid kit adding a bit of weight I probably should have forgone. I spent Sunday evening packing and Monday morning I was ready to go.

Starting from the Big Horn Crags trail head the first half mile of the Ship Island trail is up a very steep grade, and a hiker once compared the trail to a roller coaster—up and down, up and down. Many of those ups and downs are in excess of 1,000 ft., and most of the trail is between 9,000 and 11,000 ft., so it's a high altitude trek all the way. The last three miles drop rapidly to 7800 ft. Until I stood looking at that first grade, I had failed to consider that I had just spent the last five years of my life at sea level (four years in Washington D.C. and one in Honolulu). I was in for a rude awakening. Those 16 yr. old boys took off up that trail like a herd of mountain goats. I was winded before I had climbed the first hundred feet. The whole day was spent with the boys racing ahead and me plugging behind. Roy was somewhere in between. Periodically the boys stopped and waited impatiently while I caught up, but as soon as I was close enough to even consider dropping my pack they were off again. No rest for me.

After a couple of hours I began to notice that my lungs were not the only organs complaining. I had not worn boots for five years, and my feet were letting me know that they, too, were not up for this trip. Since we had not started hiking until early afternoon, we did not travel all the way to Ship Island on that first day. We camped at a small lake about eight miles from the trail head. The last mile before we arrived at that camp I developed a stabbing, sharp pain in my left knee. I was a horrible mess as I limped into camp—dead last. I had packed that over-sized first aid kit, and the only thing I treated on that trip was my own blistered feet. Surprisingly, I recovered quickly, probably due to the fact that I was in good physical shape except for acclimatization. The next morning my knee had quit hurting, and I managed to patch up my sore feet. I made it the rest of the way to Ship Island with little distress, in part because the last three miles were downhill.

Preparing packs for horses and mules was a new experience for me. One tries to keep their load between 200 to 300 lbs.—depending on the size of the animal. I soon realized that the saddle horses actually got the worst of it. Ken and I each weighed nearly 200 lbs., wore small day packs and tied a 100 lb. bag of horse pellets behind the saddle cantle. The packs on the mules and pack horse had to be carefully balanced. If too much weight is on one side the rocking and jostling on the trail will cause the pack to slowly slip. If it rotates far enough to suddenly roll under the mule's belly, the animal is likely to panic, and one is in for a real rodeo. After traveling the trail for a half mile or so, Ken would stop to assure that the packs were straight. If one side was sagging he would straighten the pack saddle and then balance the load. I thought he would do this by taking something from the heavy side and placing it on the light side, but what he did, in fact, was pick up a large rock and put it in the light pack. "Ken," I said, "that is really a rotten trick to play on that helpless animal." He laughed. "It's a lot easier than moving stuff from side to side and, believe me, that mule is a lot happier with the added weight than he would be with the cinch from and unbalanced pack rubbing the hide off his chest."

Climbing that first grade on the back of a horse was much more to my liking than hiking it with a heavy pack as I had done the times before. Ken was riding a 3 year old colt that he had just broke, and I was on a 7 year old gelding quarter horse usually ridden by Ken's wife. He was an excellent, smooth animal, and I was all smiles when we got to the top and stopped briefly to rest. Though I had ridden a great deal in my youth, I had never led a pack animal, and I had absolutely no experience with mules. I quickly learned that they are a little smarter than horses and have considerably different personality traits.

A few miles into the trail, we encountered a large, dead tree that had fallen across the path, and there was no way around it. Fortunately, Ken had the foresight to pack a small saw, so we set to work sawing our way through that tree. After a while, we stopped to rest and I heard a distinct munch, munch, munch. The mule I had been leading had managed to undo one of the straps on my saddle bag. He had lifted the corner of the flap, inserted his nose into the bag and was feasting on the apples I put there for Ken and me to snack on. Later on during that trip we tied that same mule to a tree. Again I heard him munching. This time he had a knuckle of the nylon lead rope in his mouth. By the time I jerked it free the two saliva soaked halves of that ¾ inch rope were attached to each other by nothing more than a slimy string-like filament. We spliced it and got through our trip, but on our future treks Ken used light chain instead of rope to lead the mules. On one of our trips we crested the top of one the many rises and stopped to rest. One of the mules decided he was tired and flopped down on his belly. No amount of pulling, prodding or poking got him up until he figured he was adequately rested. He then got up by himself, and we continued on without further incident. Yes, mules are different.

A few miles from the trail head the trail splits. If you take the left fork the ride to Ship Island is eleven miles. If you take the right fork the ride is fourteen. On first thought it would appear to be a no-brainer— take the left fork. But alas, there is a tiny complication. A couple of miles from the place where the trail splits there is, on the eleven mile trail, a stretch called the Beaver Slide. It probably amounts to no more than a half mile, but it goes down an almost cliff-like face. The trail is narrow with numerous switch-backs. One prays he will not meet a horseman coming the other way as there is no room to pass and no way to turn around.

My first encounter with the Beaver Slide was on my first scout trip. The scout masters had opted for that route, and when they got there the whole slide, facing north as it was, was packed with snow several feet deep. Men and boys spent hours with axes and shovels chopping crusted snow and shoveling a trail. Some of the more adventurous boys slid down on their back packs. The men finally got the horses safely to the bottom, but it was dicey. It was impossible to tell where the trail actually was under the snow, so there were places where horses missed the trail and slid down to where the trail was coming back the other way. Two men held on to a lead rope, and one man held onto a horse's tail thus keeping the floundering beast from falling and rolling to the bottom.

On this trip there appeared to be no snow on the Beaver Slide, so Ken and I opted for the shorter route. When we got to the slide and looked down the trail, it looked formidable even with no snow. The trail was only inches wide and there was no way I was going to ride a horse down it. Ken thought that was funny, but he sympathized with me, so we hiked down and led the horses and mules. On our future trips we took the fourteen mile trail every time.

As Ken rides almost daily, he suffered no discomfort from the ride. I, on the other hand, had not ridden a horse for years. My butt was chafed and my left knee ached from the slight internal rotation required to keep my foot in the stirrup. The last portion of the trail is three steep miles from the top of the mountains down to Ship Island. It is not particularly difficult as it is all downhill, but riding downhill with a sore knee is considerably worse than riding up. In spite of the discomfort one cannot help but enjoy the splendid scenery. The terrain is quite dry most of the way, but just before reaching this last leg one descends into a large basin holding two or three beautiful, small, shallow lakes within which there are no fish. Then one ascends over the far rim of the basin and views a beautiful alpine lake called Airplane Lake two miles down the trail and Ship Island Lake a mile below that.

AIRPLANE LAKE IN NEAR BACKGROUND. SHIP ISLAND BELOW

There are numerous small creeks, some from snow melt and some from springs. In my Boy Scout days, when we were thirsty, we dropped onto our bellies and drank directly from those creeks, and we filled our canteens. Giardia infection had not yet been described and to the best of my knowledge nobody ever caught an illness resembling it. Ken and I carried pumps with Giardia filters.

By the time we reached Ship Island Lake, I was more than ready to get off that horse. At the upper end of the lake, maybe 200 ft. from the water, there was a large open spot which looked like a great spot to camp. There was a creek with clean water nearby, and there was plenty of room for the horses and mules. It was right beside the trail which continued on to the lake. We set up camp, took care of the horses, and I sat on a large log to rest.

I looked up the trail and beheld an obese middle-aged woman with no shoes and no pack coming toward me. She was drenched in sweat and her chest was heaving as she greedily sucked in the thin mountain air. How in the world did this woman make it over that Ship Island trail? We exchanged pleasantries, and I invited her to sit on my log and rest. She sat and after she caught her breath she said, "Aren't you Carl Stones?" I about fell off the log. It turned out that she was Sharon Jensen (name changed) from Downey. Her father had been one of my scout masters in my youth, and I had occasionally done some work for him around his home. Sharon was considerably younger than I, but I remembered that I had never seen her at home when she was not bare foot. Apparently that aspect of her personality had not changed. A short time later two sturdy lads appeared on the trail. The older of the two, about sixteen, had his own pack on his back and his mother's pack on his chest. He had hiked almost the whole trail carrying two very large packs. That was one impressive young man!

The evening of our arrival Ken and I inflated our float tubes and fished on the upper end of the lake, but we caught nothing so the next morning, instead of fishing, we hiked around and did some exploring. Sometime later, as we were returning to camp, I stepped across a small creek (one of several inlets) near the lake, and I noticed several rainbow trout hurriedly scurry for cover. There was a large tree on the edge of the creek, so I stepped behind it, out of sight, and the trout quickly returned. I rushed back to camp, fetched my fishing pole, and then I returned and positioned myself behind that same tree. I tied on a Wooly Bugger and dropped it into the water a little upstream from the fish. As it drifted near them, they quickly scurried away as they had done when they had seen me. I lifted the fly from the water, and they returned. I tried fly after fly and it was the same story. The fish would scurry away, but quickly return once I lifted the fly. Finally, I tied on a small ant pattern. I dropped it into the water and instead of scurrying away all of the fish made a dash for it. I caught three of them before they got wise.

SHIP ISLAND LAKE

I went to the small beach where we had left our float tubes, put on my waders and fins and kicked out onto the lake near the mouth of that creek. That ant pattern was dynamite, and I was catching fish after fish. After a while, though, I began getting vicious strikes but no fish. I wondered how the heck I could be missing so many. I could see the ant each time I made a cast and it looked fine. After about 30 minutes of this I finally decided I'd better take a closer look at that fly. To my astonishment the sharp end of the hook was broken off, so there was nothing to hook fish with. The ant was still intact on the shank, so all the fish that struck were getting freebies. I'd never had that happen before, and I thought to myself, "That's what I get for using flies made in Formosa." I almost always tie my own flies, but I had tied no ants, so all I had were a few my daughter had given me for my birthday.

When we returned home I immediately tied up several ant patterns, but they were pretty sorry looking replicas. I thought I had learned my lesson and would never again fish unsuccessfully for so long without checking my fly, but, alas, I've had numerous experiences since when I casted and retrieved or trolled for prolonged periods of time and then discovered I had either no fly or I had a broken hook. It's really hard to catch fish that way.

When we were not fishing, Ken and I hiked and rode horses around the lake. From the outlet, it was only a few hundred feet to the edge of the mountain. From this point, one could see the middle fork of the Salmon River wending its way through the valley miles below. The entire panorama was gorgeous. The outlet was a large creek that quickly reached the edge of the mountain and then cascaded for miles down the steep mountainside until it reached the Salmon River.

About half way around the lake, just across from the island, there was another large open spot that made an even better camp ground than the one we had selected. There was a large area to picket the horses and a small meadow where hobbled horses and mules could graze. We camped there on all future trips.

All four of our trips to Ship Island were made during the third week of July. The trail was always open by then, but it was not unusual to encounter patches of snow that were sometimes dicey to cross on horseback. The water in the creeks and rivulets was cold enough to chill your teeth and excellent to drink. The fishing in Ship Island Lake at that time of year was always excellent, but it took us a while to find the hot spots. After the first year we kicked out to the island which was not far from our second campground and which, not surprisingly, was the shape of a ship. The best fishing was around and near the island. The fish were rainbow, cutthroat and cutbow trout. Most were ten to fourteen inches, but there were occasional larger ones up to seventeen inches. They were fat and feisty and, when hooked, did a lot of jumping.

A GOOD MEAL

They were excellent fighters and fun to catch. The ant pattern here seemed to have no special appeal. I used a variety of fly patterns and caught fish on all of them. I spent time fooling around to see how many different patterns the fish would take. On our fourth (and last) trip I made a switch to a Henry's Lake Renegade. Holy Toledo! I learned at that moment the difference between having some success with any one of many flies and then fishing with the right fly. I caught fish almost every cast—one after another after another. I had started fishing around 7 AM, and it was probably an hour or so later when I tied on the Renegade. By 10 AM I had caught and released 74 fish. Then the Katabatic wind came down through the valley as it always did about mid-morning, and I elected to quit. Late in the evening the wind had died down, and Ken suggested I go back out and see if I could get my total catch up to 100 fish for the day. It was getting pretty late, but I caught another 22 fish before it got too dark to continue. I had caught 96 fish. I've had better days since but at that time it was the best fishing I had ever enjoyed.

AUTHOR FISHING SHIP ISLAND LAKE

The fourth trip, sadly, turned out to be our last to Ship Island. The U. S. Forestry Service decided to use the Bighorn Crags Trailhead exclusively for back packers. A different trail head several miles away was designated for horses. It was 22 miles to Ship Island over that trail, and that was a whole lot more than my tender butt could tolerate. Ken suggested the possibility of camping overnight half way—two days in and two days out. I did not like that idea. It was too much vacation time spent on the trail and too little at the lake. Besides that loading and unloading horses and mules, setting up camp and breaking down camp is a lot of work. We decided that it was just no longer worth it.

# THE CHAIN LAKES RODEO

Ken and I decided we were no longer going to make the trip to Ship Island, but we were not about to give up our summer pack trip, so we searched for another destination. Ken suggested we try the Chain Lakes in the White Cloud Mountains. That idea excited me since it was another place I had been to as a Boy Scout.

It was the only place I had ever caught fish on a bare hook. Our Scout masters had actually targeted Frog Lake as our destination, but it was an easy hike from Frog Lake to the lower Chain Lakes. The lakes are so named because there are 13 of them connected by a small stream. Number one is at the bottom and the lakes are scattered up a steep, narrow valley.

CHAIN LAKES

Number 13 is at considerable elevation. Some of the lakes are quite close together whereas others are separated by a good hike. We boys made the trip in mid-July of 1952 or 1953. After spending a day at Frog Lake watching the scout masters trolling while we fished unsuccessfully off the bank (we boys got only one trip across the lake and back in the rubber raft) Thayne Vaughan, Claire Evans and I decided to seek greener pastures. Early the next morning we packed up our poles and fishing gear and set out up the trail. It was steep at first but we eventually reached the top of the ridge and then followed the trail along the top for probably two miles. The trail then dropped down the same side of the ridge a short distance to the first Chain Lake. We decided we wanted to see them all, so we kept going and we almost made it. The valley is fairly steep and one gains elevation rapidly. We did not continue to number 13 because lakes 12 and 13 were still frozen over. The ice was just recently off number 11, and when viewed from above, we could see that the shallow, crystal clear water was teeming with fish. We tied on small hooks and baited them with salmon eggs. With every cast the bait was swarmed with small Brook Trout which were so skinny they looked like snakes. I caught two or three fish, and then while I was reaching for my bottle of salmon eggs I inadvertently dropped my bare hook in the water. To my utter astonishment it was immediately grabbed. I caught a fish on a bare hook! I had heard people laughingly say that fishing was so good you could catch them on a bare hook, but they were joking. I had never before thought that it would be possible. All three of us started fishing with eggs until the fish were really swarming, and then we'd toss in a bare hook and catch a fish. We thought it hilarious.

It was getting dark by the time we arrived back in camp at Frog Lake, and we were hungry and tired. We fried those skinny fish, ate them half cooked and thought it was the best meal we had ever eaten. We made a halfhearted effort at cleaning our mess kits in cold water and then crawled into our sleeping bags.

I had purchased my bag through an off-brand catalogue for $7, and it was the worst sleeping bag on the planet. Even in those days you didn't get much of a bag for less than $25 or $30. It was made of thin, cheap olive drab material, and the batting was sparse. The quilting was poor, so the batting tended to separate and wad up. The bag had no water proof cover, and it was completely inadequate for cold mountain nights. Worse yet, I had no air mattress, so I slept on the hard, cold ground.

The Boy Scout books say that you can make a bed of tree boughs to keep you off the ground, but I think the writers must have never tried it—or at least they didn't try it without something like a sturdy rubber poncho or some other ground cover to put over the boughs. The first time I did it, I made the bed out of pine boughs. Pine needles worked their way through the flimsy cover on my bag, and it was like sleeping on a porcupine. I then tried boughs from a deciduous tree. I could feel every branch and stick through that miserable bag. If I selected boughs small enough that they were comfortable to sleep on I was down to essentially stripping off the leaves.

Anyway, minus boots I crawled into that bag fully dressed including my coat. Man, that mountain air was chilly. I shivered, my teeth chattered, and I was too miserable to go to sleep. It turned out that I was not the only one that had sleeping bag issues. After an hour or so, I found myself being shaken by Claire Evans who said, "Move over you dirty bounder." I did and he, also fully dressed, slipped into my bag beside me. It was crowded since, among other things, my bag was none too roomy but we were finally warm, and we slept well until morning. Frog Lake was aptly named. Frogs were everywhere. We spent the rest of the trip amusing ourselves by catching frogs. We inserted a hollow reed into the behinds of a few frogs, gave a small puff of air to distend their bellies, removed the reed and threw them into the water and watched them try to dive. I have no idea how facile frogs are at passing gas, but we were highly entertained by the concept of jet propelled frogs. I like to think we did them no lasting harm.

As usual, Ken and I made the trip on horses and found a wonderful camping spot on lake number 3. We set up our tent next to the water and picketed the horses a hundred feet away. We were having a marvelous time until early the second day when a young college age woman clad in a Forestry Service uniform appeared. She had a New England accent, and she was bent on letting us know who was in charge. She said we were camped too close to the lake. Tents were supposed to be 100 feet from the water's edge. Thankfully, she did not make us move it. We were not so fortunate regarding the horses. She said they had to be 300 ft. from any water whether creek or lake. Ken and I set about moving them. We easily moved the horses 300 ft. from the lake but could not distance ourselves from the numerous creeks. We'd move 300 ft. from one stream and find we were only 200 ft. from another. Places that were an appropriate distance from water were unsatisfactory for the horses. Finally, we found an almost satisfactory place, but it was a quarter of a mile from camp. We picketed the horses there because we had to, but Ken was nervous. A lot can go wrong with tied up horses and mules, and we were camped too far away to be on top of any problems.

Ken got up several times during the night and made trips to the horse picket to check the animals, and each time found them to be OK until morning when we went to feed them. Since he had last checked, one of the mules had got his back foot over the picket chain and had abraded all the skin off his hock just above the hoof. He was lame, and there was no way we would be able to use him to pack out. We were ticked. Fortunately, when the time came to break camp the animals had eaten most of the pellets, and we were able to get by with one less pack animal.

I went onto the lake in my float tube and set about catching fish. They were easy to catch, but every one of them looked like it had come from the same mold. They were all 9 inches long and had a girth about the size of my index finger. They were pathetic. Never-the-less, I learned a great deal from those fish. Ken and I threw small balls of bread into the crystal clear water near our tent, and I observed the following: If there was but one fish, it would circle the bread a few times and look it over and then gingerly eat it. If there were several fish, they would make a dash and the first one to the bread grabbed the prize. Ah, what a little competition can accomplish. I tossed a fly into the water and found the same phenomenon. Often when circling the fly a fish would bump the leader which explains what may be happening when one seems to get a strike but doesn't catch a fish. Short strikes and tail grabs may also occur, but we didn't see it here. It also explains some of the foul hooked (hooked in the head or body but not in the mouth) fish. I have a better understanding of why one sometimes gets vicious strikes and other times little half-hearted bumps. There are, of course, other valid explanations for all of it.

Ken and I made one trip to Frog Lake. This beautiful, small lake was covered on one side with lily pads that were in bloom, and the large, white flowers were beautiful. The fish were bigger and more fun to catch than those in the Chain Lakes, but there seemed to be very few of them, so hook-ups were few and far between. Since the lake was small, we covered most of it during the course of the day and never did find a concentration of fish.

FROG LAKE

There was another small lake, the name of which I can't remember, across the ridge from Frog Lake, and we fished it on still another day, and the fishing was good. It was populated by good sized cutthroat. I caught most of my fish at the inlet and outlet, but I found a deep hole shaded by a fallen log, and I pulled a lot of fish out of that.

The trip back to our camp involved a steep ride up the mountainside to the crest of a ridge and then a long ride along the top. As we concluded our fishing, a rapidly moving thunderstorm moved in, and so we rode along the top of the ridge in driving rain with lightening popping uncomfortably close. The air was heavily charged with electricity, and we anxiously rode along realizing that, atop our horses, we comprised the highest points in some places. We were very careful to keep our graphite fishing rods down flat against the sides of the horse. I kept saying to myself, "It's rare to get hit by lightning, it's rare to get hit by lightning," until I almost believed it.

While we were camped on Chain Lake 3, two men and their wives set up camp across the lake. Since the lake was small, they were not all that far away. We encountered them moving around the lake, and we chatted with them on a couple of occasions. Since the fish didn't amount to much, Ken and I spent some time riding the horses around the mountains and taking pictures. On our return from one such trip, we encountered these two couples on the trail. We chatted a bit and then one of the women said, "After you guys left camp this morning we went skinny dipping." The other woman placed one hand on her hip, the other behind her head, thrust her chest forward and assuming her best sultry voice chimed in, "Yeh, you boys missed the show." I just smiled and, without a word, reached to Ken's saddle horn and lifted off the binoculars. Then, with a smirk on my face, I stood there gently swinging them. The look on that woman's face was priceless. Ken and I had not peeked, of course, and had no idea the event had even occurred, but we didn't tell them.

On the day of departure, we broke camp and loaded our animals. The remaining fit mule was loaded a little heavier than usual. After a quarter of a mile or so, we stopped to balance his pack. It had shifted a little, so Ken loosened the cinch to straighten the pack saddle. He put a rock in the light pack but somehow got distracted and forgot to retighten the cinch. We set out, and the pack load, surprisingly, stayed put until we got about half way back to the trailhead. We were crossing a particularly rough patch of trail when, suddenly, that pack rolled 180 degrees and ended up under the belly of the mule. You'd have thought somebody had set off a stick of dynamite.

That mule panicked, and the rodeo was on. He immediately started to buck and kick. Ken was hanging onto the lead rope plowing the trail with his heels and yelling WHOA, WHOA and a few unprintable expletives. He couldn't stop the bucking, but he did keep the mule from running away, and he had the rope burned hands to prove it. That mule bucked until he was too tired to continue, and it was a good thing because Ken was almost too tired to keep hanging on. By then the pack saddle was lying on the ground, and the contents were scattered over two hundred feet. Panniers were dumped, straps were broken and packs trashed. As we surveyed the situation we both had an expletive or two to offer up.

We gathered our stuff and made a pile by the trail. We put what little we could back on the mule, but with all the broken straps it was not much. We remounted and rode quickly to the trail head where we unloaded what gear we had. Ken then saddled the mule and put one of our remaining pack saddles on his horse. He said he would ride the mule because he was smoother to ride and had more endurance for a quick ride. I stayed at the truck and did what I could to stow gear for the trip home. In a few hours Ken came trotting back to camp. We loaded our stuff and drove home in the dark.

This trip was the last I made with Ken. He had surgery on his bum knee and developed some coronary problems. I also had a bad knee, and it had become painful to ride. I miss those wonderful campouts and will treasure them to my grave. Ken will always be a wonderful friend.

# FISHING WITH JIM SORENSEN

"Carl, don't ever tell your wife you had a good time without her or she won't let you go again." These profound words of advice were offered up by Jim Sorensen as we unloaded his gear upon returning from an utterly fantastic day of fishing at the Chesterfield Reservoir. I laughed as I responded, "Jim are you trying to tell me that your wife believes you go fishing as often as you do just so you can be miserable?"

The upper end of Chesterfield reservoir extends onto the Bannock-Shoshone Reservation, and there is a line of buoys across the water marking the boundary. On good water years, there will still be water at the buoys in late summer and early autumn. The water for a hundred yards or so below the buoys will be shallow and weedy, but for some reason huge rainbow trout love residing in those weeds.

Jim and I had arrived at the reservoir early on a cloudless, September day, and I guided my boat carefully through the weeds, until I found the old river channel where the water was a couple of feet deeper. We both spooled up intermediate, sinking lines and tied on our flies. I was using two flies. I had an olive green Crystal Bugger on the end and a brown Crystal Bugger on the dropper. Chesterfield is crowded with damsel flies in the summer, and I suppose both patterns are perceived by the fish to be damsel fly nymphs—at least that's what I use when the damsels are really active.

It was a little late in the season to be thinking in terms of damsels as your "go to" fly, but I immediately started catching fish. Jim sat casting, retrieving, casting, retrieving and was catching nothing but a bad dose of frustration. He switched flies and put on exactly the same thing I had—same line, same leader, and same flies. He still caught almost nothing. Now he was frustrated and exasperated as well. "Dammit, Carl," he complained, "what's your secret?" "Jim, I swear I don't know what to tell you to do different," I said. In truth, I would have preferred for him to be catching fish also, but if only one of the two of us was going to be hooking the big guys I was glad it was me.

Late in the afternoon, Jim took off his intermediate line and spooled up a floating line. He tied on an eight foot leader (the water was eight ft. deep), placed a strike indicator at the top and tied on two chironomid patterns. He made his cast. WHAM! A 20 inch fish grabbed his fly and took off for the weeds. He then caught another and another and another—he was catching more fish than I was. It was too bad the day was almost over. He did not need the strike indicator as those trout were really slamming the flies. At the day's end we started our trip home, and we both had broad smiles. I disregarded Jim's advice, though. I bragged to my wife for an hour about catching all those fish.

Several years ago, Jim Cox and I joined a group from the Magic Valley Fly Fishers Club on a project to clean up a stretch of the Little Wood River. During a break we were standing just off the highway between Richfield and Carey, Idaho. We noticed an unfamiliar, tall, blond, gregarious man who chatted amiably with the Fly Fisher members. I noticed that he had a so-called pill rolling tremor of his hands and exhibited the dyskinesia characteristic of Parkinson's Disease. We learned that his name was Jim Sorensen, and he had grown up in Pocatello. He had been a sales executive for Les Schwab Tires, but he was retired because of his disability, and he had recently moved to Twin Falls. I liked him immediately and, after chatting with him for a while, invited him to accompany me fishing when I took my boat out.

I expected that he would require some help when preparing to fish as tying knots and tying on flies requires considerable fine coordination, but Jim turned out to be full of surprises. He could tie knots as well as anyone. He controlled the tremor in his hands by clamping his elbows and forearms tightly against his ribs. Fly casting by some fishermen can be called "Poetry in motion" but such was not the case with Jim. His casting was downright ugly. The muscular rigidity of Parkinson's Disease made it impossible to start and stop his casting motions with precision, so his line sort of slopped back and forth, but he managed to get his fly into the water, and he could lay out a good amount of line.

Usually, when setting the hook into a fish, one lifts the tip of the fly rod and pulls back quickly on the line. When Jim hooked a fish he lifted the tip of his fly rod alright, but it was sudden, violent motion and it just kept going. The tip of his rod flew high into the air and back over his head. It reminded me of the motion I used as a youngster when I flipped chubs over my head. I half way expected to see a fish go flying, but Jim had a good, flexible fly rod instead of a rigid stick. I thought it fortunate, at times, that he had a backrest on his fishing chair to keep him from going over backwards.

When he got excited his dyskinesia got worse, and he was always excited when he hooked a fish. At times his calf muscles began to twitch, so that his knees bounced up and down and his hips wobbled from side to side causing the boat to rock. I accused him of making me seasick. In spite of his affliction, Jim was a very good fisherman. He knew where to fish, and he understood how to fish so he was successful more often than not. Since Jim was retired he was generally available to go fishing, so he and I spent a lot of time together on the water and became fast friends.

We did not always fish from my boat. Jim had a pontoon boat with a small electric motor, and I had a float tube which we used on small reservoirs such as Daniels near Malad, Idaho. Fishing from a tube is, in many ways, superior to fishing from a boat. One can turn in all directions, move a few yards one way or the other, work between the weeds and, generally, fish with a little more stealth. A main drawback to tube fishing, especially for us old geezers with hyperprostatism, is developing a full bladder out in the middle of a lake. It can cause a frantic kick back to shore at times, and the bladder spasms that occur when relief is anticipated occasionally causes an unwanted dribble or two. Jim was considerably younger than me, so he couldn't blame anything on his prostate but, if the fish were biting, he, like unto me, stayed on the water until he was truly desperate before he made his dash. Once he got to shore he had to unbuckle his waders and push them down in order to get at his zipper. With his tremor and the rigidity of his hands he had a hard time with both. As his anxiety increased his dyskinesia got worse, and his hips began to sway back and forth. I could read the degree of his desperation by the wobble of his hips. I occasionally sat grinning thinking about how I was going to rag on him if he peed his pants after making that desperate dash, but he somehow always managed to get the job done.

Before he had ever been there, Jim had heard both Jim Cox and I talking about the phenomenal fishing at Daniels Reservoir. He wanted to go fishing with his brother-in-law, and he thought Daniels might be a great place to try, since it was not too far away. I gave him directions on how to find the place, and, in late August, he and his brother-in-law set out, towing the brother-in-law's boat.

As they pulled off the highway near the reservoir, they noticed a wooden outhouse just ahead of them on a small hill and to the left there was a boat ramp descending a steep incline. Thinking they had arrived, they drove down the ramp and to their dismay discovered that it ended well before it reached the water. The ramp was at the end of a small bay and extended into the water only when the reservoir was full. Determined to somehow get their boat into the water, they turned to the right and drove along the side hill just above the water, until they found a spot where the lake bottom appeared rocky enough and firm enough to support the weight of their pick-up. They maneuvered the truck so that they were backing straight down the hill and then descended, rolling the boat trailer into the water.

Just as they got far enough to float the boat off the trailer, all four wheels of the truck sank to the axles in mud. The truck was in four wheel drive but the incline was steep, and they couldn't move any way but down and farther down was definitely not where they wanted to go.

As they set out to find help, they climbed the 100 ft. incline, stepped over the crest and there, immediately in front of them, was the main boat ramp the end of which was well into the water. Had they driven 50 ft. beyond the outhouse instead of taking the first ramp, they'd have seen it immediately and saved themselves a whole lot of trouble. They found another fisherman with a truck who was willing to help them, but he was completely baffled as to why they had tried to launch in the mud with a perfectly good cement ramp just a few feet away. With a lot of digging, swearing, packing ruts with rocks and a tow from the congenial fisherman, they finally were extracted from the muck. Finally, with the boat properly launched, they managed a few hours of fishing but it was an off day and as a conclusion to all the crap they had been through, they didn't catch any fish.

Though I grew up fishing creeks and small streams, I am not much of a river fisherman. I greatly prefer still water. Jim, on the other hand, loved to fish moving water, and he occasionally asked me to go along. One October he asked me to make a trip with him to fish for German browns in the Owyhee River. We took his camping trailer and stayed for several days.

Jim had acquired a Labrador pup that he named Remington, and he and the dog became inseparable. The dog slept in his bedroom at home, and if Jim went fishing the dog went fishing. He folded the back seat in his truck down and laid a thick blanket over it. That was Remington's place. If you rode with Jim, you could expect a wet, canine nose in your ear or a warm muzzle on your shoulder as you traveled. Remington, of course, accompanied us to the Owyhee.

Because of his Parkinson's Disease, Jim had to rest frequently. When he got tired his dyskinesia worsened, so he would quit fishing for an hour or so. He placed a chair outside the trailer, and he sat there to put on his waders to get ready to fish. He left his street shoes by the chair. When he needed to rest, he would quit fishing, return to the chair and read for a while or slump down in the chair and nap. On our second morning, Jim returned to his chair and discovered that his shoes were gone. Completely puzzled he searched the camp site. He looked in the trailer wondering if he had absentmindedly put them there. No shoes. He was about to find me to ask if I had moved his shoes and then it struck him. REMINGTON! Shortly later, I returned to the trailer and was surprised to find the usually tranquil Jim thoroughly agitated. "Sometimes," he fumed, "I wonder why I have a damned dog." After I managed to quit laughing, I helped him look for his shoes. We found first one and then the other out in the sagebrush a considerable distance from the trailer. We were actually a little bit lucky to find them both. They were covered with slobber but otherwise none the worse for wear.

Early one morning I left the trailer and walked to the river. I looked down into the clear water and discovered a large, male German brown lying in a small pool. His tail was gently oscillating—enough to keep him from floating down stream—but he was otherwise not moving. Greatly excited, I dropped to my hands and knees hoping the fish would not see me and crawled closer to the water. I tossed my fly into the water above his hole and floated it down to him. He paid no attention. I did it again and the fly just drifted right past him. I did it over and over, sometimes dropping the fly close to the pool and sometimes a ways upstream. Sometimes the fly even bumped him on the nose, and he paid no attention. I'd never seen such an unperturbed fish. I couldn't get anything to work. I changed flies, but the results were the same. I went through fly after fly. Nothing, it seemed, enticed the fish and nothing disturbed him.

Finally, I tied on a small green fly. I don't even know the name of it. I dropped it in the water above the hole. It drifted past the fish and was ignored just as all the others had been. I tried again. Same result. I was discouraged and ready to give up, but I decided to give it one more try. I dropped the fly into the stream, and the fish exploded out of his hole and slammed that fly like a freight train. My jaw dropped, and I was so surprised I almost dropped my pole. "gottcha, you son of a gun," I muttered gleefully. He headed out into the current and took off downstream. I wasn't about to lose him after all that effort, so I spent several minutes playing him, and just as I was getting him into the net Jim appeared for one of his rest periods. I held the fish while Jim snapped a picture, and then I eased him back into the water. The next morning I returned to the river and the big brown was back in his hole looking as if nothing had happened. I didn't bother him again.

AUTHOR WITH OWYHEE GERMAN BROWN

120

I have often wondered what there was about that one pass that enticed the fish. Nothing looked different to me but something surely looked different to him. It makes me wonder how many fish ignore our fly presentations for every one we catch.

On another occasion, Jim persuaded me (it didn't take much) to accompany him to the Big Wood River near Bellevue, Idaho. That river runs through so much private property that access is difficult except at the public access designations. At the first place we planned to fish, we parked in the designated area. We made the considerable hike to the river and discovered four persons working the holes upstream and two more fishermen downstream. We drove to another public access, but the situation was similar. All the holes were being worked by someone. The third place we stopped we lucked out—there was no one else there. We had to hike through a wooded area to get to the river. I started walking downstream, and as I broke through some brush I noticed a huge, sweeping bend in the river. Near the far bank there was a deep hole, and, wonder of wonders, fish were rising. "Man," I thought, "this is going to be sweet."

I stepped back into the brush and worked my way, unseen, within casting range. I stepped slowly out onto the gravel beach and was just beginning my false casts when I heard a bit of commotion, and I looked back to see a school teacher and about 15 kindergarten children emerge from the trees. The kids immediately sprinted to the rocky beach and began to entertain themselves by throwing rocks into the hole I thought I was going to fish. The teacher flashed me an innocent smile and, without further ado, waded into the water and began overturning rocks looking, I suppose, for critters to show the kids. It was apparent that I was not going to catch any fish there. With resignation I waded upstream to another hole and made a few casts. I waited around thinking the teacher and the kids would eventually move on, but they seemed planted for the duration. I suppose they must have moved eventually but it was well after I was gone.

One fine fall day Jim and I went fishing on the Salmon Dam Reservoir. We fished Whiskey Slough most of the morning with considerable success. At noon we ate our lunches and then moved a short ways up the reservoir and resumed fishing. A short time later, Jim began rapidly reeling in his line. "Carl," he said, "I'm sorry but

I've got to take a crap—bad!" I reeled in my line, pulled in the anchor and fired up the boat. "Hurry," Jim pleaded. His jaw was clenched, and his face reflected an urgent desperation.

We were at least two miles from the dock, so I thrust the throttle forward and we roared down the reservoir. I barely bumped the dock and Jim jumped out and started for the toilet which was above the top of the ramp about a hundred yards away. He ran as fast as he dared but between his dyskinesia, the necessity to keep his sphincter clamped and the uphill slope it was an uncoordinated, rapid waddle. He was working at the buckles on his waders as he went.

When he finally disappeared into the outhouse, I backed away from the dock and ran across the reservoir to some cliffs. There are times when some really nice fish hang out at the base of those cliffs, so I threw out my anchor and began to fish. After a while I began to worry. Jim had not emerged from the privy. I was about to pull up my anchor and go check when the outhouse door opened, and Jim stepped out. I was relieved, but it looked like I needed to return in any case, so I reeled in my line, lifted my anchor and turned toward the dock to pick him up. He got about a third of the way down the ramp when he suddenly whirled and ran back up the hill.

I killed the motor and sat for a bit, but when he did not immediately come back out I turned around and tossed out the anchor. Sometime later Jim emerged from the crapper again. I lifted the anchor and started for the dock. This time Jim got about half way down the ramp when he turned and once again made a dash. I didn't know what to do. Once again I sat for a while then turned and went back to the cliffs. The third time Jim emerged from that edifice of relief I stayed where I was until he was more than half way down the ramp. He kept coming so I then pulled up the anchor and returned to pick him up. I was about to ask him what in the world happened when he grinned sheepishly, stepped into the boat and said, "Ahhh, I feel so much better now." It was all I needed to know.

The sun was just beginning to touch the mountain tops. Jim Sorenson and I figured we had a little less than an hour before it got too dark to fish, but we planned to take full advantage of the time that we had. It was a beautiful summer evening, and we had already been on Magic Reservoir for several hours without experiencing a whole lot of success. Never-the-less, we had thoroughly enjoyed ourselves. Jim was always fun to be with, and that particular day he had been in fine form. If laughing is good for one's health, we should both have added several years to our lives.

Jim was sitting on the bow seat, and I was standing, fishing near the stern. I made a long cast off the rear of the boat and was facing rearward. Suddenly I heard a loud "POP" about like a .22 shot followed by an equally loud curse from Jim. I spun around and, for a moment, was a bit puzzled. Jim looked as if he had suddenly gained 50 lbs. Then I burst out laughing. It was not until that moment that I realized Jim's fishing vest was inflatable. When he had made his cast, he had snagged his reel on the rip cord that released the $CO_2$ cartridge. He looked like the Pillsbury dough boy.

I had not known until then that inflatable fishing vests were available, but what a fine idea. At my next opportunity, I bought one for myself. I always wear a fishing vest anyway, why not one that doubles as a life jacket? I now wear it whenever I am in my boat, but what I like best is that it fulfills the requirement some states have to wear a life jacket when out in a float tube. I am exceedingly careful to make sure the rip cord is stowed in such a way as to be almost impossible to snag. The vest came with two $CO_2$ cartridges both of which I dearly hope I never need.

When Jim and I returned from our fishing trips, as we parted company, he would invariably shake my hand and say, "Well, Carl, we cheated death again." A few years ago Jim and his beloved dog were returning from fishing the Sublett Reservoir. He took the first Twin Falls exit and was on Kimberly Road headed toward his turn-off at Addison Avenue. He was less than 10 miles from home. Just as he approached the Hansen Bridge, his pick-up suddenly drifted into the oncoming lane and took a semi head on. He and Remington were killed instantly. It appeared he had fallen asleep, but no one will ever know exactly what happened. Unfortunately, he did not cheat death that day. I have often wondered why Jim did not ask me to make that trip with him. Would my being along have kept him from going to sleep or prevented whatever other error occurred? Would I have been killed also? Unanswered questions. What I do know for sure is that I lost a very good friend and fishing partner that day, and it saddens me still.

# HUMILITY SUCKS

Gifford Springs has a special place in my heart. A few years ago, while fishing there, I hooked three fish with tags in their dorsal fins. One of the tags was worth $50, and the other two tags were $25 each. It was the only time in my life I got paid for fishing.

The Gifford Springs are on the upper end of the Walcott Reservoir. Many years ago, before the Walcott Dam was built, these large springs were alongside the Snake River and served as an important source of cold, clean, fresh water for travelers emerging from the sage brush desert. Now, of course they are under water. In the heat of the summer fishing becomes poor in much of the Walcott reservoir as fish go deep seeking cool temperatures, but many large trout find their temperature needs met in the cold water around the springs. It is a place where one can often find superb fishing during the summer doldrums. The existence of the springs is certainly no secret, though, so there is always the risk of making the 70 mile trip from Twin Falls and finding boats already parked in the good places. All you can do in those situations is move over into the weeds, hope to find some bass and hang around and hope somebody moves.

One hot August afternoon Jim Cox and I arrived at Gifford Springs and, to our delight, found no one else there. We launched Jim's boat, headed across the lake and tossed out the anchor in our favorite spot. To successfully fish the springs, it is usually necessary to get one's fly right down to the bottom of the lake, so we strung our rods with fast sinking line and tied on bugger type flies weighted with a few wraps of lead wire. You pay a price in lost flies, as the reservoir bottom consists of large basalt rocks. Snagging a rock and breaking your leader is a frequent occurrence, and many a fly, lure and baited hook has rusted away wedged in the cracks and crevasses in those rocks.

Jim got his pole strung up faster than I did and made his first cast. He counted his fly down to the bottom and began his retrieve. He had made only a few pulls on his line when a smashing hit nearly jerked the rod out of his hands. His slack line immediately disappeared, and his reel began spinning. A very large rainbow erupted from the water, shook vigorously and hit the water with a resounding splash. "FISH

ON," Jim yelled with a gleeful laugh. The fish headed back toward the boat, and Jim reeled furiously trying to keep the slack out of his line. The fish swam under the boat, took off again, and once more Jim's reel began to sing as the line disappeared. Jim somehow kept his line away from the anchor rope and maneuvered it out from under the boat without losing the fish. Finally, the fish began to tire, and Jim began to make some headway as he reeled it in. I stood with the net poised, but as soon as the fish saw the net it took off again. Ultimately, I netted the fish, and Jim slipped the hook from its jaw. "That's not bad for a first fish," I understated. A few casts later, I hooked a fish and we replayed a similar scenario. We started catching one large fish after another.

We were so engrossed in our fishing we did not notice when another boat drew near, and we did not pay it much attention. Within the boat were two young men fishing with spinning rods and power bait. They parked a respectful distance away and began casting toward our hole, but they didn't catch anything. They pulled up their anchor and moved a little closer. Jim and I continued to haul in the fish, carefully returning each one to the water. The young men could not even get a bite. They watched in awe, and finally one of them said, "Gee, you guys really know what you are doing." Jim and I smiled at each other as our egos soared. Our heads probably swelled three hat sizes. Absolutely nothing is better than catching fish when the guys next to you can't. After some time, feeling magnanimous, we moved and let the young men have our spot. We moved to where they had been. We continued to catch fish and they continued to get nothing, and our egos rose even more. Man, we really knew what we were doing! Those guys were fawning all over us. By the time it was getting dark, and we needed to quit fishing, we were feeling really full of ourselves. We had Gifford Springs fishing knocked.

We returned home, but we could not get Gifford Springs out of our heads, and we could hardly wait to go back. "Man, you guys really know what you are doing" replayed through our heads like a circular magnetic tape. When I went to bed that night I even dreamt about catching those big fish. Two days later, we were gleefully on our way back to Gifford Springs, and we arrived at the same time of day as we had previously. There were other fishermen on the lake, but our luck was good, and there was no one parked where we wanted to fish. We threw out our anchor, strung our rods exactly as before and tied on the same flies. Our expectations were high as we began our casts. One cast—two—a dozen casts—no fish. We made cast after cast and could hook nothing but those basalt rocks, and we were very proficient at hooking those. We were absolutely baffled. We began switching flies. Still we caught nothing.

After about two hours of disappointment and disbelief Jim said, "It's obvious that those trout have moved out. I wonder why? Where do you suppose they would go?" I had no clue. We sat pondering what might have happened to those fish, and a small twelve foot aluminum boat holding three large men pulled up next to us. It was fortunate that the water was calm because they were so crammed into that boat they could hardly move. "How's the fishing," they asked? "Terrible," we replied. "We did well two days ago, but for some reason the fish have moved out," Jim complained. The guys took their time stringing chironomid patterns on about ten feet of leader topped with a strike indicator.

The first guy made a cast. Wham! He barely got his hook into the water when he hooked a fish. The second guy made his first cast. Wham! Another fish! Jim and I sat with mouths agape, feeling rather sheepish. What happened to, "Man, you guys really know what you are doing?" Obviously, the fish had not moved. chironomids were one thing we didn't try. Why the fish wanted buggers two days ago and only chironomids today had us scratching our heads. Fish can be really finicky at times.

As we sat and watched those guys pull in fish our egos plummeted, and our heads shrank back to our natural hat sizes. Talk about a lesson in humility. We both had lots of chironomid patterns, and we were just kicking ourselves knowing that we might have enjoyed fine fishing had we just given them a try. We started tying them on but, by then, the strangers in the row boat had pretty much depleted the hole so we still didn't catch any fish. Those guys showed us the patterns they were using, and they even gave us three of them. We didn't catch anything with those either. Obviously, when fate sets you up for a dose of humility nothing is going to bail you out. I am not, by any stretch of the imagination, an artist when it comes to tying flies, but the flies those guys gave us were pretty sorry looking by even my standards.

The fish did not seem to care. I took those patterns home and tied up what I thought were pretty respectable looking versions, but to this day I have never caught a fish with any of them. Humility sucks!

# HENRY'S LAKE

"Did you see the moose and her calf as you drove to Staley Springs this morning?" Bill Schiess asked as he anchored his boat near the edge of one of the well-known Henry's Lake holes. "Cast over near those weeds." I made the cast and began my retrieve. "I did," I replied, "but I almost missed them because it was still a little bit dark. I was going to—WHOA!" My pole bent double. The line I had retrieved flew from the bottom of the boat. My reel began screaming as the line disappeared, and then the backing began peeling off. I tried to enhance the drag by placing my thumb on the reel, but all that won me was a quick friction blister. Within moments my backing was getting dangerously low. Bill dropped his pole onto the bottom of the boat and leapt to the control panel. He started the motor and began to follow the fish. "Don't give him any slack," Bill yelled. No problem. My backing was still disappearing albeit at a slower rate. Suddenly, my line went slack, and I began cranking the reel furiously, hoping the fish had turned. Bill stopped the boat and I cranked the slack out of my line only to discover that my fly was solidly anchored to something, and it wasn't a fish. "He got into the weeds," Bill lamented. He inched the boat forward as I reeled in my line, and then I began to pull—gently at first and then more firmly. Just when I thought I was probably going to break the leader and lose my fly the obstruction gave way, and I lifted from the water a huge wad of weeds—an all too common story when one hooks a Henry's Lake hybrid.

There is no fresh water fish quite comparable to the Henry's Lake hybrid. It is a cross between a female Yellowstone cutthroat of the type endogenous to Henry's Lake and a male rainbow (I don't know what strain). They are incredibly strong, and they grow very large. Fish in excess of ten pounds are not uncommon. Whereas a hooked cutthroat will pull downward and try to go deep and a hooked rainbow is likely to leap and run, a hooked hybrid will invariably take off like a rocket, ripping line off your reel. They may leap also, but it is their strength and endurance that makes them thrilling to catch. You simply cannot horse a large hybrid into your net, and it takes time to wear them down. These fish, in my view, are the main attraction to Henry's

Lake, but there is also absolutely nothing boring with catching the large cutthroat or trophy sized brook trout that abound.

One summer I hooked a large hybrid, and it took off. It ripped all my fly line off my reel and was well into the backing when my line suddenly went limp. I wound my backing back onto the reel and discovered that the knot holding my line to the backing had come apart. I lost my whole fly line! On another occasion, I hooked a hybrid, and it took off so fast the retrieved line I had on the bottom of the boat flipped up and formed a nice half hitch around two of my fingers. I shook my hand violently trying to free my fingers, but I was too slow. That knot cinched down, the leader snapped, and the fish was gone. One day I was fishing and a sudden squall arose. I began running the boat forward trying to keep the nose into the waves, but I was still dragging my line. Suddenly one of those hybrids struck and began ripping line off my reel. I didn't know what to do—play the fish, try to keep my line out of the propeller and risk swamping the boat or steer the boat and lose the fish. I opted to play the fish, but it soon got off the hook anyway. It was probably fortunate since I didn't get swamped. Never-the-less, I was ticked about losing that baby. Those fish are dynamite. I am not the least bit unhappy when I hook a cutthroat or a brookie but it is the hybrids that keep me going back to Henry's.

There have been two occasions when I have snagged fishing line while fishing Henry's, and when I pulled the line out of the water found it still attached to some unfortunate souls rod and reel. Were these losses the result of an engagement with a couple of those hybrids? Obviously, there are greater misfortunes than losing one's entire line. One of those rigs had been on the bottom for a long, long time, and it was so crusted with sediment and debris that it could not be cleaned up but the other one made a nice set-up for a grandson.

Henry's Lake is a large, shallow reservoir about four miles long and three miles wide. It is near the Montana border at the edge of the Island Park Country. The lake is only twenty three feet deep in its deepest part when the reservoir is full. One often does his fishing in six or seven feet of water. There is a small dam at the outlet, and the lake drains into the Henry's Fork of the Snake River. Because it is shallow, weed growth is abundant, and the weeds sustain a huge population of aquatic insects which, in turn, grow very large fish, and the fish grow very fast. The lake is fed by several small creeks and a few large springs. These areas as well as open water between weeds are called "holes", and if one is to be consistently successful at fishing Henry's Lake it is necessary to know where the holes are and precisely where to position one's boat or float tube. GPS devices have revolutionized the ability to do this, but previously it was necessary to get aligned with certain landmarks in two different directions. This alignment process caused me to make one of the most embarrassing mistakes I've ever endured while fishing.

The Henry's Lake State Park camp ground is second to none in beauty and grandeur. It is one of my wife's favorite places to camp, so for many years we went there for three to five days several times each summer. Clea does not like to fish, so when we were camping, I generally went onto the lake by myself. I occasionally acquired, when I could, the services of Bill Schiess on my first day out. Bill had guided on Henry's for many years, and he knew the lake about as well as anybody on earth. By going out with him, I could learn on the first day where the fish were located, so when I went out alone on subsequent days, I was likely to be more successful. After a few trips, we got to be pretty good friends which made my gaffe' all the worse.

On one of my trips, Bill was booked for the whole week, so I went onto the lake by myself. Near the south end of the lake there are a series of holes, Phil, Cobb, and Barrel holes, which are in a line and are only a few feet apart. On this day, I decided to try those holes, and eventually I settled into the Cobb hole. The fishing was fantastic, and I spent several hours there. Around noon, Bill came cruising nearby, stopped and asked me how I was doing. "Oh man," I replied, "it is incredible."

Bright and early the next morning I headed back out onto the lake planning to plant myself in that same hole, but when I got to the general area, there sat Bill in his boat with three clients. I guess it was one time when I had showed him where the fish were. For some reason, I assumed he was in the Barrel hole which was a few yards southeast of Cobb. I circled past him, and began checking out the landmarks for the Cobb hole. I aligned myself with the landmarks to the south, and then began backing the boat while watching the landmarks to the west. Finally, looking south and west, I found myself aligned both ways. I cut the motor and turned toward the east to throw out my anchor—and there was Bill's boat not ten feet from me. I was practically sitting on his lap. He raised his hands in an "I don't know what you are doing Carl, but it isn't going to work" gesture. My jaw dropped, I muttered an apology, fired up my boat and moved to the west. I was so flustered that I didn't really think about where I was moving to. I was just eager to get out of his casting lanes.

There were two things I knew for sure about Bill: (1) he believes (rightfully) that boat movement spooks fish in shallow water, and (2) he does not like to be crowded when out with clients. I was guilty on both counts. I was now a respectable distance from him to the west, but I was not in a hole. I went through the motions of fishing but caught nothing. When I finally settled down and got my wits about me, I decided to move south of Bill. I thought I was far enough away to be a non-problem to him, but as I Idled southward I heard him gripe, "Right around my boat he goes." I felt about two inches tall. My southward position turned out to be a sweet spot, and I ended up glad I moved. I caught a lot of fish while Bill and his clients seemed to be doing poorly. After about three hours, I decided to move on and leave the area to Bill so I called, "See you later," and as I pushed the throttle, I heard him grumble, "Not if I see you first." I was dreadfully embarrassed by what I'd done, and the next time I saw Bill, I apologized profusely. He just laughed and said, "Aw, it wasn't that bad." Thankfully, we remained friends. One good thing that came out of the experience aside from catching some nice fish was that, ending up in Bill's lap as I did, I now knew for sure that I had my Cobb hole landmarks right.

I first fished Henry's Lake with Jim Cox. We were fishing from my small 12 ft. double-hulled boat. I was using the old flies I had tied up in my fly tying class some 15 years earlier in Spokane. The fishing was phenomenal, and those old flies were working just fine. There was actually about a half hour when I caught more fish than Jim did, and I thought I'd really arrived. At the end of the day, though, Jim's tally at least tripled mine.

There were many other occasions when Jim and I fished the lake together. Being shallow, as it is, the water gets warm in the summer time, and the summer doldrums is very real. Our favorite time to fish Henry's was in the fall. We've been on that lake when ice kept freezing on the eyelets of our rods, and we had to keep dunking them into the lake to melt it off. We've fished it in float tubes when snow was blowing sideways and pelting out faces. Almost always, though, we were catching fish.

On time, Jim, Bob Norman and I were fishing on a very cold day, and we were all bundled up in winter clothing. A stiff wind came up, and we decided it would be wise to get off the lake. I had a boat slip rented at Wild Rose, so I turned into the harbor and pulled into my boat slip just as another boat passed behind me. Jim lifted one foot onto the dock, and just as he went to step out of the boat the wake from the other boat heaved up the front end and catapulted him across the dock and into the water on the other side. Man, was he cold! Bob and I were laughing so hard we could hardly pull him out of the water.

Even in the summer, fishing Henry's can be treacherous, and it is necessary to keep an eye on the weather. In that Island Park country sudden, violent storms can form up and strike within just a few minutes. I've sat in my trailer and watched the wind rip tent pegs out of the ground and roll the tents, with all their contents, clear across the camp. Stories abound about fairly large boats that were flipped because their owners did not get off the lake in a timely manner.

One summer I was fishing with my son-in-law on what started out to be a nice summer's day. When we launched the boat, Hyrum stood on the dock and held onto the 50 ft. rope I have tied to the front. There is a compartment at the front of the boat for stowing the rope, but instead of using it, Hyrum piled the rope on the deck. The fishing was slow and we had not had much luck. Hyrum had snagged weeds and lost several flies. The fish he did hook either broke off or got into the weeds. I had not done much better, and we were entirely frustrated. We had fished for several hours, trying hole after hole, when one of those sudden squalls struck, and we were on the opposite side of the lake from the boat launch. Fortunately, the wind was coming from our rear as I worked my way back. I was at the controls and was gunning the boat over the wave crests and cutting back to slide into the troughs. It was imperative that I did not let the boat get turned sideways as those waves were huge.

Suddenly, I noticed that there was no rope on the deck. It had washed into the water. My heart nearly stopped. Fifty feet of rope, tied to the front end was dragging behind the boat. If that rope got tangled in the prop, we could possibly have a quick lesson in what big trouble really is. "Hyrum," I yelled, "get that rope stowed." He stumbled toward the bow and began to pull the rope in hand over cumbersome hand. He was having a considerable problem trying to retrieve the rope and hang on to the pitching boat. I was sweating bullets worrying that the prop might catch that rope or Hyrum might be pitched overboard. After what seemed like an eternity, he lifted the end of the rope over the side and, to my palpable relief, stuffed it into the storage compartment. He crawled to the rear of the boat, sighed loudly, and plopped himself onto the seat. I successfully navigated the huge waves and returned to the dock. I am usually reluctant to quit fishing and take my boat out of the water, but I was actually glad to get my boat onto the trailer that day.

There are lessons to be learned on any water, but some of my observations at Henry's almost made me think that some of my previously held beliefs were myths. One of those was the belief in short strikes. On many occasions when one is retrieving a fly there will be a small tug, or perhaps a series of small tugs, on the line. The belief is that a fish is grabbing the tail of the fly (short strike), but not getting enough of it to get hooked. I'm sure this sometimes happens as one can, at times, shorten the tail a bit and improve the catch rate. One day at Henry's I was making a retrieve, and I felt bump, bump, bump. "Ah, short strikes," I thought. The water was crystal clear, and as my fly got close to the boat I could see a large cutthroat rapidly swimming around and around the fly looking it over. Each time it passed in front of the fly it bumped my line, and I felt a small tug. I've since witnessed that same phenomenon at the Chain Lakes and at Dierke's Lake, and I believe that many of the bumps attributed to short strikes are actually fish bumping the line while examining the fly. I think this also explains why some fish get foul hooked.

Another belief is that the passing of a boat or a float tube in shallow water will spook the fish away. That is certainly true in many situations—especially when the fish have really been pounded by fishermen. One day I was fishing Henry's Lake in the channel of

Staley's Spring near the big bend. There were boats all around me. I was using two flies, a Hot Chocolate on the end and a Henry's Lake Renegade on the dropper (both are Bill Schiess creations). The fishing was excellent, but I was experiencing a situation I was at a loss to explain. I would catch fish on the end fly only and nothing on the dropper for a prolonged period of time, and then the fish would switch and I would catch them all on the dropper. After some period of time, there would be a brief lull and then the catch would switch back to the end fly. Very puzzling, but it's not the only time I've had it happen. Anyway, I was catching all these fish when I see a guy in a tube working his way between boats. He was circling right past me in such a way as to float over about 50% of the water I was working. It really ticked me off. Overcome with a diabolical urge, I decided to cast my line across his tube to see if that didn't, maybe, give him the idea he was a little too close. Fortunately, I missed, and my fly fell just beyond his fins. He was looking over his shoulder as he was kicking backwards and didn't see it. I started my retrieve, and as the fly passed immediately behind him I hooked the biggest fish I caught all day. The tuber kicked merrily on his way completely unaware. Moreover, I continued to catch fish. The tuber's passing did not seem to affect the fishing at all. I have been in similar situations, though, when a boat or a tuber passed by and it would be a half hour or so before the fish moved back and one started catching fish again.

Bill Schiess has a great sense of humor. He made a good portion of his income by tying flies, and he called his fly tying business "BS flies." I think a fly tying business is as much about hooking fishermen as it is about hooking fish, so Bill invented a new fly for each season. He was very good at it, and he knew what worked on Henry's Lake so, of course, his flies caught fish, and the word would spread that there was a new hot fly. We fishermen all had to have it. I tie my own flies, but I had to buy the new ones so I knew what to copy. His patterns are excellent, so I use them extensively on many other reservoirs with great success. There are at least five of his patterns that I would not be without: Henry's Lake Renegade, Mity Mouse, Hot Chocolate, Crystal Buggers (light olive, dark olive) and Electric Black.

Clea and I usually departed for our camping trips on Monday morning, but on one occasion in July, for reasons I have long since forgotten, we left home on a Sunday. At that time I had a Ford 250 pick-up, and I was towing a 27 ft. Cobra fifth wheel. I had my 12 ft. double-hulled boat on the boat carrier atop my truck. We had just passed Idaho Falls, and I had sped up to 65 mph when I saw an old Cadillac rapidly approaching a stop sign at the edge of the highway. My foot twitched toward the brake but the Caddy stopped. Just as I breathed a sigh of relief the woman driving it quickly glanced to the right and then shot out onto the highway directly in front of me. I slammed on the brake, but there was no avoiding a collision. I smacked her left rear door and spun the Caddy 360 degrees. It was fortunate that she was in that big, heavy car because she was uninjured. Clea and I also avoided injury. I got out of the truck to check out the damage. There appeared to be no serious structural problems, but the grill was bent and the radiator punctured so the truck could not be driven. My boat was still atop the truck, but the rack was bent, so it sagged down in front of the windshield.

Eventually, a tow truck arrived and pulled us to a repair shop where the truck and trailer remained for three weeks. The trailer sustained only minor damage. Two of the tires were worn flat on one side from the brakes locking up. Clea and I loaded all our coolers, food products and valuables into a rental car and made a somber trip home, aggravated that our camping/fishing trip had been derailed but happy that we were uninjured. The elderly lady who caused the accident was hurrying because she was late for church. That's what I get for going camping on Sunday!

# CHESTERFIELD LUNKERS

Jim Cox eased his boat through the mats of weeds toward the west shore of the Chesterfield Reservoir a few hundred feet below the buoys marking the Indian Reservation. Small, scattered patches of open water were present, but we were looking for the old Portneuf River channel. Suddenly, the water depth dropped from six to nine feet. "Jim," I said, "I believe we have arrived." "What a pleasure it is to fish with such a perceptive partner," he replied, as he tossed the anchor near the edge of the weeds.

It was a late August morning, and bright, blue Damsel flies were flying and alighting on the boat, on our fly rods, on us, just about everywhere. Many were locked in copulation to brown females. I tied an olive Crystal Bugger, which is an excellent Damsel nymph simulation, on the end of my tippet and a brown Damsel nymph on my dropper. "Here fishy, fishy, fishy" Jim called as he made his first cast. I made my cast immediately afterward. Almost instantly, our rods bent double and large rainbows exploded from the water. "Fish on," we whooped simultaneously. "Man, Jim, you've got that fish call nailed today," I said. Jim remained at the rear of the boat, and I fought my way to the front. "Oh please no," I pleaded as my fish headed towards Jim's line. I was trying to put the brakes on, and Jim was trying to horse his fish away from mine. "You keep away from me," he laughed. We were struggling to keep the fish from crossing our lines and getting tangled, but it was almost impossible to stop them from going where ever they wanted. We managed to turn them, and Jim finally got his fish to the boat and released it, but mine got into the weeds and broke off. I was upset.

My discomfiture did not last long, though, because all morning long, and all afternoon we caught those fish. When it seemed we had worn out our welcome in one place, we'd move a few feet to another patch of open water and start over. We caught 40 or 50 fish apiece. Almost all were greater than 18 inches, many were more than 20 inches, and they all were of thick girth and very strong. I've had occasional days when I've caught more fish, but never one when they were all so consistently large. As we fished, an occasional boat farther down the reservoir would turn toward us and come ripping our way full throttle—until they got to the weeds. The boats would abruptly stop, and the drivers would look those dense mats of weeds over and discuss the situation with their companions. About all we could make out of their conversation was, "How the hell-----?" With a shake of their heads they would then turn their boats around and go back down the reservoir. Jim and I cracked up every time. Tilting the motor up and pulling off a few handfuls of weeds from time to time was a small price to pay for catching the beauties we found hiding there.

Not every day of fishing at Chesterfield is quite so spectacular. There are, in fact, days when you get skunked. The first time I fished Chesterfield, I had only recently started fly fishing. I was at the reservoir by myself, fishing from my float tube. I kicked around the lower end where I had seen some bank fishermen catch a fish or two. I managed to catch only a few fish, but at that point in time I thought I was really becoming a master fly fisherman. With great expectations, I returned a few days later with my boat, accompanied by my nephew to whom I had been extolling the wonders of fly fishing and boasting about the great fishing at Chesterfield. I made a great show of demonstrating how to string up his pole, tie knots to attach his leader and tie on his fly. I then proceeded to catch absolutely nothing. Not even a nibble. My nephew, who had never fly fished before, caught two nice rainbows. He was, of course, completely delighted and felt as if he had completely out fished me. The Gods of fishing fed the old uncle a large dose of humility once again.

With all fishing there is a huge element of luck associated with success. Fish are not everywhere in a lake, and one tends to be much more successful if one fishes where the fish are as opposed to where they are not. The first and most important challenge is to find the fish. This is made complicated by the fact that fish don't bite all the time. If you are not catching anything, does it mean the fish are not where you are fishing, or they are there but hunkered down? If one can spend from dawn until dusk on the water, there will usually be some period during the day when the fish are feeding, but that is not always true, and when it is true, the bite may be of short duration.

There have been many times when I have fished for hours and thought the fishing was really crappy, and then they started to bite, and I left the reservoir with a smile on my face and went home feeling like the fishing had been really good. If the fish are biting, and the fish are where you are fishing, you still have to choose the right fly and fish at the right depth. If you are lucky enough to hit all those parameters right, you will probably catch fish. Jim Cox and I have had days when we moved from place to place, hole to hole until we finally found fish that were biting, and then we spent the rest of the day hauling them in.

On some occasions we spent the night at a nearby ranch and could hardly wait to get back out on the water the following morning. Then morning came, we arose at the crack of dawn, ate a quick breakfast and headed back onto the water ahead of most of the other boat traffic. We wanted to make sure we got our spot. With great anticipation, we returned to where we had enjoyed success the day before, threw out the anchor, put on the same flies, made the same casts and failed to stir up so much as a bite. The fish had either moved, or they were not feeding. It has happened more than once. Again we may spend the day moving from place to place, and maybe we find fish, and maybe we don't. Maybe they are just not biting and nobody is catching anything. How can the fishing be red hot one day and absolutely dead the next? Fishing is a fickle sport. Exhilaration may turn to frustration or vice versa, but we return home with the memory of when the fishing was great, and that is invariably what we remember when the question of returning to Chesterfield comes up.

The Chesterfield Reservoir is a 1600 acre impoundment[4] about equidistant from Lava Hot Springs and Soda Springs Idaho. The upper third of the reservoir is on the Fort Hall Indian Reservation. There is a string of buoys across the reservoir to mark the boundary. The reservation water cannot be fished unless one obtains a license from the Indians. Chesterfield is rich in aquatic insect life as well as snails, leeches and other food sources. The trout grow fast and large, and the reservation end provides a huge refuge where they are relatively untouched. The reservoir is fed by the Portneuf River. During the summer when the reservoir water warms, large trout move into the cool river water on reservation property. Those who know where and how to fish it and have a reservation license can catch very large fish. While fishermen without a reservation license cannot fish the extreme upper end of the reservoir, in the spring, weeds and willows extend about a quarter of a mile or more below the buoys, and late in the season, when the water has been drawn down this becomes the upper end. Those who learn to navigate through the weeds, in the late summer and fall, and fish the patches of open water can sometimes do very well.

Less than a half mile from Chesterfield Reservoir there is a large ranch. At some time in the past, the owners conceived the idea of starting a dude ranch. Their idea was to give a few city slickers an opportunity to ride horses, work cattle, do ranch work and pay for the privilege. They built a bunk house which is actually four very nice rooms in a row, much like a small motel. Somehow their idea never matured, and they began renting the rooms to fishermen. The accommodations are very nice, but all of the ground water in the valley is saturated with hydrogen sulfide, and the well water smells like rotten eggs. It is safe to drink if you can get it past your nose, and the ranchers and their families are all used to it, so they cope. When we stayed in those rooms, we drank bottled water. Whenever we ran tap water, flushed a toilet or took a shower the bathroom stank of $H_2S$, but it was tolerable—really not much worse than a world class fart— and the rooms were otherwise very comfortable.

Jim Sorenson and I fished Chesterfield one October afternoon and spent the night in one of the ranch rooms. Our plan was to get onto the lake early the next morning. We arose at dawn and discovered that it was very cold. The sky was clear, but dense fog had settled into the valley. You couldn't see ten feet, but since the day was cloudless we figured the fog would soon burn off. We had left the boat beached and tied to some willows the night before, so we boarded my pickup and slowly groped our way through the fog from the ranch to the boat dock. We wanted to fish the upper end of the reservoir, but it was about a mile from the dock, and we could hardly see from one end of the boat to the other. We formulated a plan: We would aim the boat up the reservoir and slowly troll until we got to the weeds, and there we would anchor and wait for the fog to lift. We pushed the boat into the water and climbed aboard. I started the motor and headed across the reservoir until I figured we were safely away from the dock, and then I turned toward the upper end and we began to troll. After about twenty minutes I saw something looming just ahead of me in the fog, and I quickly cut the motor. To my amazement it was the dock! I had run the boat in a great big circle, and we were right back where we started from. Jim and I decided that maybe we had best just stay put and wait for the fog to lift, so I headed out a hundred feet or so from the dock and pitched the anchor. Jim and I froze our butts and fished while awaiting the sun. We expected to catch nothing where we were anchored, and our expectations were met.

The fog lifted about 10 AM, and Jim and I headed up into the weeds and began fishing the old river channel right where, on an earlier trip, I had enjoyed spectacular success while Jim caught nothing. To our bitter disappointment, there was no action for either of us. We moved into a large bay a little ways down the reservoir, and Jim began catching fish. We were running the boat in close to the shore and then drifting toward deeper water. Jim was picking up two or three fish every drift, but I couldn't seem to manage so much as a nibble. Jim was using a four sink line, and I was using a three. I figured I could just count down a little longer before beginning my retrieve, but it didn't work. I changed lines, and I still caught nothing. The fishing was not red hot but Jim continued to hook up regularly. I wanted to move elsewhere, but Jim was happy where we were. It didn't bother him in the least that I couldn't catch anything. I was tempted to remind him that it was my boat, and I could darned well move it if I wanted to, but I restrained myself. I couldn't deny that fish were present. When we quit fishing at the end of the afternoon, I was in a sour mood, but he was jubilant. He really enjoyed the turnabout. As I said before, fishing is a fickle sport.

On the last day of October one year, I was fishing with Jim Cox and Bob Norman. Since it was Halloween, I decided it made perfect sense to tie on a Halloween leech pattern. On the first cast, I nailed a big rainbow, so I stuck with that fly all day. I insisted that the Gods of fishing had inspired me and were amused by my choice. In any case, it was working as well as anything Jim or Bob tried. Late in the afternoon I hooked an eighteen inch rainbow that had a phenomenal girth. It had taken the fly deep, and it was into its gills. I removed the hook as carefully as I could, but the fish was bleeding badly, so I decided to keep it.

There was no problem figuring out what that fish had been feeding on. When I squeezed its abdomen I could feel and hear the crunching of snail shells. That fish was full of them. I took the fish home, butchered it, baked it and tried to eat it. It was terrible. I've eaten trout in the past which could be described as "fishy" or "mossy" tasting, but that fish exceeded them all combined. Neither my wife nor I could choke it down. Even the dog didn't like it. Since that day I have never kept a big trout to eat. If it is larger than 14 inches, back in the drink it goes, and the rare ones I do keep have to be out of cold, clean water and completely devoid of snails.

There are occasions when plans do not materialize as expected. Sometimes, if one is lucky, the outcome may be even better than the original plan. One July I wanted to fish Chesterfield. I called Jim Cox on Sunday evening, and he wanted to go with me, but he was not available until Tuesday afternoon. I decided I would drive to Downey on Monday, spend some time with my sister, Una, my brother, John, and his wife, Dorothy. I would spend the night in Downey, then drive to Chesterfield (about 45 miles) on Tuesday and spend the day fishing. Jim would join me Tuesday evening, and we would spend the night at the ranch bunk house, fish all day Wednesday, and and then return home.

I towed my boat to Downey and visited as planned. After a wonderful afternoon and evening with my sibs, I spent the night at John's place. My plan was to get up early and slip away as unobtrusively as possible, but Dorothy arose and insisted on fixing me breakfast. Gosh, what a disappointment! I ate like a pig, and after I was thoroughly sated with ham and cheese omelet and pancakes, I bid my farewells, hopped into my truck and sped toward Chesterfield.

I was happily cruising toward Lava Hot Springs when it hit me like a thunderbolt—I forgot to put my bag with all my flies in the truck. It was sitting on the floor of my garage in Twin Falls. Usually, I have a half dozen or so flies on the wool patch pinned to my fishing vest, but just a day prior to leaving home I had removed them all and put them back into their boxes. I was now about 20 miles from Chesterfield, and I had absolutely nothing to fish with. I pulled to the side of the road and called Jim with my cell phone. I asked him to swing by my house on Tuesday afternoon and pick up my bag. That did not solve my immediate problem. I had seen some flies in a service station convenience store near Lava Hot Springs on a previous trip, so

I figured I could pick up something there to get me by, but I was out of luck. They had a few dry flies and nothing else. The manager told me he had a shipment of flies due in a couple of days. I stopped at a couple of other service stations. None had flies. I decided to drive to Soda Springs. I figured that it may be a large enough town to have a fly shop. It was 20 miles from Lava Hot Springs and entirely out of my way, but I made the drive. I hunted and asked around and finally found the town's only fly shop. Elated, I parked and ran to the door. It was closed. A sign on the door said the owner was ill, and the store would not be open. I sat in the parking lot fretting over my rotten luck and wondering what to do. I decided there was nothing I could do but drive to Pocatello, fifty miles away.

I made the drive and arrived at Sportsman's Warehouse at 9:20 AM. The store did not open until 10:00, so I sat outside and fretted and waited. The morning was almost shot. When the store opened, I rushed inside and grabbed a few buggers and damsels. The only damsel pattern they had was brown. I retraced the thirty mile drive back to Lava Hot Springs and turned north toward Chesterfield. Fifteen miles later, I arrived at the lake. I launched my boat and was on the water at noon. I raced up the reservoir and turned into a large bay which is separated from the main body of water by a long, shallow ridge. I eased over the ridge and into the weedy bay. I threw my anchor into some open water and pondered which of the new flies to use. Usually when I use damsel nymphs at Chesterfield, I use either olive or green, but, having no other options, I chose brown. I made my first cast toward the weeds. Wham! I had a nice fish. I released it and cast again. Another nice fish! That damsel pattern looked like it just might be alright. It was, in fact, superb.

When the fish stopped biting where I was parked, I moved a little deeper into the bay and drifted across open water catching fish after fish. Jim joined me around dinner time, and we spent the evening enjoying fantastic fishing. We stayed at the ranch bunk house and returned to the same bay the next morning, and we fished all day with spectacular success. This was one time when the good fishing repeated itself on the second day. I now had my bag of flies from home, but I continued to use the Sportsman's Warehouse brown damsel. When I returned home I tied several copies of it which I frequently use at

Chesterfield to this day. It was almost worth all the driving and the trip to Pocatello for what I learned.

OCTOBER AT CHESTERFIELD

Jim Cox is a very witty guy and can usually be counted on for some good natured nonsense. When returning from one of our Chesterfield safaris, we stopped for dinner at a Flying J truck stop restaurant. The place was extremely busy, and the waitresses were all really busting their humps. Jim and I walked to one of the few vacant tables, but it was covered with crumbs. In his best mock indignation, Jim exclaimed, "Would you look at this? They haven't even wiped off the table. What kind of a place is this?" He did not realize that a waitress was standing right behind him. As we seated ourselves, she stepped to a counter and picked up a damp rag. She immediately returned and made a great show of brushing the crumbs into a huge pile—and then, with a flourish and a very pleased with herself grin, she pushed them all onto Jim's lap. I cracked up, and the waitress held up her pad and pencil as if waiting for our order. Jim did not know whether to squawk in protest or to laugh. He just sat for a moment with his mouth hanging open. I explained later why she did it, and he laughed also. The lesson we learned that night—don't mess with a truck stop waitress.

# RED HOT DANIELS

Jim Cox and I had fished Daniels Reservoir in our float tubes just about all day. We had started at the upper end and worked our way down. Now I was fishing the far side, across from the boat ramp, and I had to pee. I mean I *really* had to pee. When I fish from my float tube, I usually accomplish this urgent bodily function by kicking to water shallow enough for me to put my feet down and stand on the bottom. I can then pass the little can I carry in a pocket on my tube down inside my waders and obtain wondrous relief, and nobody can see a thing. The lake could be wall to wall with women, and it would make no difference. Unfortunately, I was in deep water. I kicked to the far shore, but the bank was steep. I was becoming increasingly desperate. I reeled in my line and kicked down along the shore hoping to find a shallow spot or a place where I could climb out. Finally, I found a small ledge jutting out from the bank. It didn't amount to much, but it was sufficient for me to get my feet onto it and stand up. I laid my pole across my tube and removed the can from the pocket. The fly on the end of my leader was dangling into the water not more than three feet away.

I had both hands inside my waders, when suddenly my rod flew into the air, and line started ripping off my reel. Fortunately, the reel snagged momentarily on a strap. I had a can full of pee inside my waders that I didn't want to spill, but I darn sure didn't want to lose my pole. I ripped one hand out of my waders and made a grab for my rod which caused my feet to slip off the ledge. I held desperately onto my rod while that fish was ripping out line, and, with the other hand, eased the can out of the top of my waders. The spillage was less disastrous than it might have been. I dumped and stowed the can and then placed my full attention on the fish. I finally managed to get it into the net, and it was very large—the first fish I had caught all day. I could only shake my head in amazement. That large fish grabbed my fly which was not three feet away from me and dangling only inches into the water. Truly phenomenal, I thought.

I started back across the reservoir because the evening was late. As I entered the shallow water by the near shore, the sun was starting to set, and the fish were beginning to rise. Soon they were popping out of the water like popcorn, and as soon as they started to rise they began to bite. For the next hour, before it got too dark to fish, Jim and I hauled in one fish after another. It was a very hot finish to what had been a slow day.

I grew up in Downey. Chesterfield was only 45 miles to the north and Daniels about 30 miles southwest, and I had never fished either reservoir as a kid. I had to wait until many years later to be introduced to these fine fisheries by my friends in Twin Falls. My first few trips to Daniels were made within the first couple of years after I started fly fishing. I caught but few fish, but they were large, and I thought I was in heaven. It was sometime later when I gained some experience and had learned the reservoir that I fully realized what a truly fine fishery it was, and it became one of my favorite places. Since it is only a few miles from the Utah state line, it is also heavily favored by fishermen from Utah. Jim and I often joked that we needed a Utah license to fish it. The reservoir is small, only 375 acres, but either the Fish and Game Department or the Dept. of Reclamation (I'm not sure which) owns part of the water, so the farmers are not allowed to drain it dry. There is good carryover each year. In addition to heavy damsel hatches and the usual array of aquatic insects, there is a robust population of fresh water shrimp. Trout grow fast, and they grow large. It is a trophy reservoir and can be fished only with flies and artificial lures. The limit is two fish, and they must be longer than 20 inches.

One day in July, Jim Cox and Bob Norman were fishing from Jim's boat, and I was nearby in my float tube. We were on the upper end of the reservoir, and Jim and Bob were parked in the old creek channel. I would kick toward them until I got almost into their casting range and then turn and kick back toward some dead trees and willows which were about 200 ft. away. Once back at the trees, I turned toward the lower end of the reservoir and fished along a line of willows. I had been back and forth several times and was getting discouraged when, suddenly, the fish began to bite. It was as if someone had thrown a switch. Jim and Bob started hauling them out of the channel, and I was catching them near the willows and weeds. I caught 60 fish and then, about mid-afternoon, someone threw the switch the other way, and the bite stopped. It was the first time I had ever caught that many fish in one day.

As I stated earlier fish don't bite all the time. Some days they bite for only short periods. If you give up in disgust because you are catching no fish, you will leave the lake griping that the fishing was crappy. If you happen to be on the lake when the bite is on, even if you have fished for hours without catching anything, you leave with a smile thinking the fishing was wonderful. This, of course, all pre-supposes that you are fishing where the fish are, but just because you are not catching them does not always mean they are not biting.

On one occasion, I had been fishing for hours and catching very little, and I was discouraged. I then saw a guy sitting in his tube, ten feet from the bank, and he was hauling them in. He was fishing with chironomids. Most of the time when a fisherman uses chironomids, he also uses a strike indicator, which is why I don't use them much. For me, much of the appeal of fly fishing is the almost constant activity, find the fish, cast and retrieve, move around, cast and retrieve. A strike indicator is the fly fishing version of a bobber. You cast it out and then sit and stare at it, waiting for it to move. You could go blind that way. It is as near to sitting on the bank, in a lawn chair, with your pole propped, drinking coffee as you can come when fly fishing. How can you be fishing with a coffee mug in your hands? On the other hand, when chironomids are all the fish are taking, and you have a fish on the line most of the time, you get as much movement and activity as you could ever desire.

There are two guys from Ogden Utah who are regulars at Daniels. They park their campers and stay for weeks at a time. They have been there nearly every time I have fished the place, and they probably know the reservoir as well as anyone could. One day one of them was in his tube in 27 ft. of water just off the boat ramp. He had a strike indicator on the end of his fly line and beyond that a 27 ft. leader. The strike indicator was rigged so it would slip down the leader when he pulled in a fish. He had a chironomid on the end and two more at about 2 ft. intervals up his leader. He was dangling the end chironomid near the bottom of the lake. He caught 50 fish in just a few hours. Those of us using buggers and nymphs were catching nothing. It was enough to make a convert out of me, but I tried it a couple of times, didn't catch anything, and I nearly fell asleep staring at the strike indicator.

There are times at Daniels when the fish will take nothing but chironomids, but my "go-to" flies are an olive damsel pattern with a yellow tail and either an olive and black or yellow and black variegated scud resembling the fresh water shrimp. I place the damsel on the end of my leader and the scud on my dropper. These work well most of the time. One summer day, Jim Cox and I were sitting on the tailgate of my truck at noon eating sandwiches. A guy from Rupert, Idaho pulled his tube out of the water nearby, fetched a sandwich from the cooler in his truck and sat on his tailgate. We engaged in pleasant conversation. When we finished lunch, we began pulling our tubes back toward the water. "Man," the guy from Rupert said, "I hope the fishing picks up. I only caught one fish all morning." Somewhat surprised I replied, "I caught twenty." He looked at me with disbelief. I smiled, knowing he thought I was lying.

We climbed into our tubes simultaneously and kicked out away from the bank. I had barely made my first cast when I had a fish on. A couple of casts later, I had another. "What flies are you using," the Rupert guy asked? I told him and gave him a couple. I continued to get one fish after another, and he continued to get nothing. "What line are you using," he asked? I told him and showed him how I had my leader and dropper rigged. He changed his line. He fished all afternoon and evening right alongside of me, using the same set-up and the same flies. I hammered the fish, and he caught one only once in a while. "Man, Carl, these fish are going to be glad to see you go home," he said.

I have no explanation for why I caught fish and he didn't. He seemed to be fishing the same way I was. I'm sure it had nothing to do with superior skill on my part. It is just one of those unexplainable things that will happen when fishing. I have never seen that guy again, but it is entirely possible that had we fished side by side again he would have caught the fish, and I would not.

Jim Sorenson and I were fishing on the upper end of Daniels one beautiful spring morning, working our way slowly down the reservoir between the willows. We had caught a lot of fish and were enjoying watching the blue herons carrying food to their chicks in nests high up in the dead Aspen trees. The adults were making frequent trips, and with each return the heads of three or four chicks, previously unseen, appeared above the edge of the nest and competed noisily for the food offerings. One poor chick appeared to have been abandoned. It was alone in its nest, was making a constant, pathetic racket, and its head did not disappear. It kept it up for hours, and we never did see an adult. We could only speculate as to what might have happened to its parents.

Suddenly, we heard a thththththth sound, and we looked toward the water. There, about 15 feet from the boat, was a large dragon fly. It was on the surface of the water but could not fly off. It was not for want of trying. The beating of its wings against the water was making the thththth sound. It sounded like a miniature motor boat. It was trying desperately to reach something to climb onto, and my boat was the closest object. It beat its wings mightily and moved toward the boat, but it quickly fatigued and had to rest. Each time it rested, the mild breeze pushed it back away from the boat. As soon as it was able, it beat its wings again. Each time it was gaining a little ground. It was sort of a two steps forward, one step back drill. On its fourth attempt, I extended the tip of my pole toward him. He needed just another inch or so to begin climbing, and WHOOSH, there was a break in the surface of the water, and mister dragon fly was gone. Some fish got a large meal. Often, observing the other life at the reservoir is as much fun as catching the fish.

One evening I was on the upper end of the reservoir in my tube as the sun was going down. I looked across the water, and, in the middle of the reservoir, I saw what I thought was the strangest float tube ever created, and it was approaching me. It drew closer, and I thought maybe the tuber wanted to talk to me. Suddenly it became apparent that it wasn't a float tube. It was the head of a moose with a large rack of antlers, and it was coming directly toward me. About the time I decided I needed to make a run in the other direction, it either saw me or smelled me. It turned abruptly and swam all the way back to the far shore. I guess he was even more worried about me than I was about him. I was astonished by its swimming ability. That was the first moose I saw at Daniels, but I've seen them frequently since, especially in the spring. They usually are on the upper end, wading in shallow water, eating the exposed weeds.

One day I met Jim Sorenson at the reservoir. He was accompanied by two friends, and they were (ahem) on the chubby side. We all had float tubes, and there was a stiff breeze blowing from the dam toward the upper end of the lake. Jim and I battled the wind and stayed near the shore where we had parked our trucks. The other two guys soon fatigued, and, for reasons I will never understand, decided to quit kicking and let the breeze take them where it would. For a while, they were obviously enjoying themselves, trolling along, catching an occasional fish, expending no effort, but soon they were way up the reservoir with the wind pushing them into the weeds and into water too shallow to work their fins. I was highly amused as I watched them thrashing around, trying to work their way back to deeper water, only to be pushed back into the weeds each time they got their feet off the bottom. They were expending plenty of effort now. Finally, after some loud discussion back and forth, they worked their way through the mud to the bank and climbed out of their tubes. They took their flippers off, washed off the mud, picked up their tubes and other gear and began the long walk back. About a quarter of a mile from the trucks, there was a small rivulet about three feet across and three feet deep running into the reservoir. One guy tried to jump across. He gave a mighty leap, but his pudgy body chose not to leave terra firma, and he lit face down in the middle of the creek and got his waders full of water. He came out cussing and sputtering. They ended up walking upstream to a place where the bank was not so steep and waded across. They arrived back at the trucks thoroughly bushed and did not even try to fish the rest of the afternoon. Had I known them better, I'd have thanked them for the best entertainment I'd had that week.

At Daniels Reservoir it is a rare day of fishing when one does not see an osprey, but I've never discovered where its nest is. Frequently, one sees it diving like a rocket toward the water. More often than not, it lifts off with a fish in its talons. One day I was fishing in my float tube, and, nearby, I saw a very large, dead fish floating belly up. It was bloated to about twice its normal girth. Suddenly, I heard a resounding WHUMP. It was almost like someone had struck a kettle drum. I turned and saw the osprey with its talons hooked in the bloated carcass, thrashing away, trying to lift it off the water. It was much too large. After a few moments, the osprey gave up and flew away.

One warm, autumn day, I drove to Daniels Reservoir. The water was low, so I drove down the boat ramp until I was near the water, and then I pulled off onto the dried, rocky shore to park. Just as I shut off the motor, I detected a dreadful stench which was filling the cab of my pick-up. I quickly exited the truck and walked around to the right side. There, right next to my front wheel, was a dead fox—a very, very dead fox. It was swarming with maggots, and the stench was overbearing. I got back into my truck and moved to the other side of the boat ramp. I rolled down the windows to air out the stench while I launched my float tube, and then I closed up the truck and began to fish, kicking slowly along the shoreline.

A small, white van drove to the top of the boat ramp and parked. A driver and a passenger disembarked, and the passenger walked to the back of the van and opened the rear doors. Three large dogs shot out of the back. The passenger then continued on around the van, and he and the driver lit cigarettes and began conversing. I could hear them laughing from where I was on the lake. Two of the dogs ran off into the weeds, relieved themselves, and began to frolic. The third dog, a black lab, dashed down the ramp toward the water. Suddenly its head swung sharply to the left, and it planted all four feet, skidding to an abrupt stop. He hesitated a moment and then turned sharply to the left and trotted to the dead fox. He buried his nose into the rotting carcass and spent a few moments thoroughly inhaling that fine scent. Then he lay down on the stinking remains and began to roll—back and forth, back and forth. He moved onto his back and squirmed and wiggled some more. He arose and again buried his nose, then once more flopped over onto the carcass and wiggled. He acted as if he just could not soak up enough.

By this time the guys up by the van had finished their cigarettes, and one of them whistled. All three dogs dashed back to the vehicle and leapt into the back. The passenger closed the van and returned to his own door. Man, were those two guys in for a rude surprise when they closed themselves into the van with that lab. I wondered how far they would get before they made the nasty discovery—eau de rotting fox, possibly a few maggots, and one black dog badly in need of a bath.

# HUMILITY AT HAWKINS

A few weeks after my nephew, Scott Benson, humiliated me at Chesterfield Reservoir I took him to Hawkins, and he did it to me again. At that time, I had not been fly fishing very long, but I was getting to the point where I could occasionally make a decent cast. I had been going to Roseworth quite frequently and catching my limit, and I was still at the stage where I thought catching my limit was a good day of fishing. I thought I was getting pretty darned good. Twenty plus years later I look back at that time and laugh. I haven't really got good even yet.

This trip was only the second time Scott ever had a fly rod in his hands. I was still showing him how to tie on his fly. We kicked out together and began making our casts. I was making long casts, counting the fly down, making my retrieve and catching nothing. Scott was barely able to get his fly into the water. He slapped it down about fifteen feet in front of him, let it sink, made a couple of pulls on his line and WHOA! He had a fish. I was happy that he was catching fish but entirely frustrated by my failure. I had supposed that I was the fly fisherman. What was wrong here? For some reason, it didn't dawn on me that the occasional fish I did catch took the fly at the end of my retrieve.

What was wrong was that I really didn't know much of anything about fly fishing. It was sometime later before I figured it out. For Scott, it was a matter of doing the right thing by luck. For me, it was a matter of learning a little bit of fishing entomology. If the fish are taking critters that swim horizontally in the water such as damsel nymphs, pulling your fly through the water horizontally is the right thing to do. Many nymphs, though, leave the bottom of the lake and swim directly to the top—either straight up or at a roughly 45 degree angle. When fish are after those, that is how you need to manipulate your fly. At times the fish are selective, so you have to also have the right pattern, but there are times when the only important thing is the presentation. On many occasions, I have finished a long retrieve and had a fish hit just as I started to lift my line to start a new cast—just as they did that day at Hawkins. Scott was probably catching fish because, with his short casts, his fly was rising from bottom toward the surface just as soon as he started his retrieve. Short casts are sometimes the right thing to do.

Hawkins Reservoir is a small impoundment about 15 miles or so west and slightly north of Downey, Idaho and about 15 miles north of Daniels reservoir. My earliest knowledge of Hawkins was as a teenager. My dad's friend, Fonzo Dewey, went fishing one day and pulled a five pound trout out of that pond. Word of that fish was all over town before night fall. Fon's fish was almost as sensational in Downey as was the cougar he shot in the hills near Malad City a couple of years earlier. He posed with that cat near the city park until it became too dark to see. It seemed like everybody in town turned out to have a look. Folks were pretty much satisfied to just hear about the fish, but after Fon caught it, everybody with a fishing pole headed for Hawkins. A friend and I went there and joined the crowd of wormers fishing from the bank, and I caught exactly nothing, a not at all unusual experience for me in those days. I didn't fish that reservoir again until I made the trip with my nephew, and I wasn't all that thrilled about the fishing after that trip either.

A couple of years ago, Jim Cox had been fishing Daniels Reservoir for a few days. When he departed for home, he decided to take a short cut by driving the dirt road over the hills and through the wheat fields to Hawkins. He stopped to chat with a tuber just coming out of the water and found that he had done very well and caught some really nice fish. Jim decided he didn't need to get home as early as he thought he did, so he put on his gear and went fishing.

After Jim returned to Twin Falls, he simply could not wait to return to Hawkins, so just days later he, his brother-in-law Tom Schultz, and I arrived at the reservoir about mid-morning, and I got humiliated once more. The humiliation this time wasn't so much related to the fishing as it was to my stupidity. After all these years of fishing, and all the experience I've gained fishing in the weeds, I made a critical mistake. The water was very low, and the upper end of the reservoir was choked with weeds. Jim put on his gear and headed right for them. Since he had recently fished the reservoir, one would think that the smart thing to do would be to follow him, but I got it into my head that we should spread out, so I headed directly across the pond. Tom, with infinite wisdom, followed me, and we fished willows and weeds on the far shore. We caught some really nice fish, but they were few and far between.

Finally, after hours of not doing much, Tom and I exercised our keen powers of observation and noted that Jim was really hammering the fish, so we headed for the weeds on the upper end. Unfortunately, we had wasted most of the day. The water was shallow, and the weeds were so thick they were miserable to kick through in a tube, but if you dropped your fly into the scattered holes in the weeds you were rewarded with some very large fish. Jim finished the day with a huge grin on his face. Tom and I finished the day mentally kicking ourselves. We'll be back, though.

# THERE ARE NO SALMON AT SALMON DAM

I anchored my boat in 25 ft. of water near the cliffs at the mouth of Whiskey Slough, and my two grandsons began their awkward casts. I had taken Alex, age 12, to a kiddy pond a couple of years earlier, and he had caught several nice trout, but Isaiah, also age 12, had never been fishing. I was somewhat worried. I had caught a large number of small mouth bass at this spot just a few days earlier, but one never knows how the fishing will be from one day to the next, and the way my luck usually runs the fish are bound to have lock jaw if I have a grandchild with me. It was usually like that when I took my kids fishing also.

I was doing my best to instruct the boys, but their casts were uncoordinated and not much line was going out. Alex is tenacious, and he would have fished all day just for the fun of trying to cast, but Isaiah was beginning to get discouraged. Suddenly, his pole bent. "I'VE GOT A FISH," he screamed. Sure enough, he landed a nice 15 inch bass. His next casts were much more enthusiastic. Within moments, Alex also hooked a bass, but it was only 6 inches. Isaiah was not above gloating. Within a couple of hours, both boys had caught six bass apiece, most of them nice fish, and they were ready to quit. The ride home was jubilant and, after the bragging about their fish was over, the main conversation was, "Grandpa, tell us another story about when you were a boy," and grandpa, who is admittedly "full of it" was happy to oblige.

What most of us locals call the Salmon Dam Reservoir is officially named the Salmon Falls Creek Reservoir. I suppose there may have been a time in the past when salmon migrated up the creek from the Snake River to the falls (wherever it is), but that was before the dam was built. I suppose one could argue that there are salmon in the reservoir if one counts kokanee. When I first moved to Twin Falls around 25 years ago, there was a robust population of kokanee in the reservoir, and they were nice fish. Catching a kokanee weighing 3 lbs. was not uncommon. At some point, the Fish and Game Dept. quit putting them in there—perhaps because too many of them ended up as walleye food. In any case, I have not seen a kokanee out there for many years.

The Salmon Dam reservoir fills a deep, narrow canyon which has steep, basalt walls. The reservoir is 14 miles long,[5] and, when full, is over 100 ft. deep near the dam. It cannot be drained dry, and I have never seen less than 70 ft. of water in the large bay near the dam. It can be a tough reservoir to fish, and I have been skunked (or nearly so) there more often than any other place I've fished in recent years. On the other hand, the fishing can be spectacular.

It is a fun place because there are many times when you make your cast and wonder what you will pull out. You may catch a trout, small mouth bass, walleye, yellow perch, crappie, pike minnows or suckers. The pike minnows and suckers are rare, but the other species are common. The reservoir is a trophy walleye fishery, and fish larger than 30 inches have been caught.

WALLEYE NETTED AT SALMON DAM RESERVOIR
BY FISH AND GAME DURING SURVEY

The Salmon Dam Reservoir is the only one I know of where daphnia are an important food source for the trout. The food base in recent years seems to have increased or changed because trout have become more common, and the trout, walleye, bass and crappie all grow large and fat. The increase in the trout population may be due, in part, to efforts of the Magic Valley Fly Fishing Club to stock the lake with cutbow hybrids. On many occasions when a bass is hooked, it regurgitates a large crawfish. I've never had a 50 fish day on that reservoir except a couple of times when crappie were biting, but I have caught more than 20 fish many times.

On a warm May evening, when the reservoir was full, Jim Cox and I boated toward the upper end of the reservoir where two creeks join, and the water was shallow. We had hoped to catch Walleye, and we were fishing with large, black buggers with red tinsel in the tail. We pulled up next to a basalt cliff and began casting toward the rocks. The hoped for walleye were not there, but we started catching crappie, so we changed to smaller flies. I continued to use black for my bottom fly, but I put a small chartreuse fly on the dropper. We caught crappie by the dozens, and they were fairly large—for crappie.

A couple of days later I returned to the reservoir alone early in the day and was fishing about six miles upstream from the boat ramp (which is near the dam) and about four miles below where Jim and I had fished. I was expecting to catch trout or bass, but I had not caught many of either. After a couple of hours I drove up the reservoir a ways above Norton's Bay and anchored next to a cliff that had a sharp point jutting out into the water. I cast toward the point, and, just as my flies began to sink, I had a solid strike. I thought I had hooked a big fish, but when I stripped my line in far enough to see what I had, there was a large crappie on both the end fly and the dropper. Between the two of them, they put up a pretty good fight. I sat in that spot for over two hours and caught what seemed like a jillion of the little beggars. There seemed to be an inexhaustible supply. I have never again been into crappie like that at Salmon Dam. I catch one incidentally now and then but never in great numbers. It is all about being in the right place at the right time, and it helps, of course, when they are spawning.

Shortly after my daughter got married, her husband expressed an interest in going fishing, so I took the two of them to Salmon Dam. He had a spinning rod spooled with six pound test nylon line. He tied a big, red spoon onto his line, and we began to troll. It was not long until his line had twisted and kinked until it was almost unusable. I suggested that he might fare better if he tied a small swivel onto his line and then snapped the spoon onto that. He clipped off the spoon and held it in his left hand while he released some of his line and let it untwist. He then plucked a swivel from his tackle box and tied it onto his line. Recently married, as he was, my daughter was something of a distraction to him. He was paying far more attention to her than he was to rigging his pole. He completed tying the swivel onto his line and then tossed the contents of his left hand into the water. Unfortunately, he had failed to attach the spoon. He realized his mistake just as he let it go, but there was nothing he could do but sit with a sheepish look on his face and watch it sink.

Most of the time I fish the upper half of Salmon Dam, but there is nothing more aggravating than spending the time and burning gas to get miles up the reservoir only to find the fishing is slow and then making the return run toward the dam and finding great fishing not five minutes away from the dock.

One such place where the fishing is sometimes great is a narrow finger of water extending about a half mile outward from the main body of the reservoir. It is called Whiskey Slough. It is one of those places where you never know what you will pull out of the water, but it is, at times, especially good fishing for trout and bass. One day in late October, the weather was unusually warm. I went fishing alone, and I slipped down Whiskey Slough to the shallow water at the far end. It was late in the season, but I wanted to see if the bass were still biting. With little in the way of expectations, I began my casts. To my utter delight I found myself amidst a large school of rainbow, and most of them were 17 or 18 inches. I caught those beauties until my arms ached, but, eventually, I wore out my welcome or the fish moved elsewhere.

I decided to run up the reservoir another couple of miles to Antelope Bay. It is a structure very similar to Whiskey Slough, but not as long. Similarly, I drove to the far end of the bay and anchored in 12 ft. water. Again I found myself hauling in rainbow. I fished until I decided I had done enough for one day, but I left the reservoir with the thought in mind that I was going to return very soon. I could not wait to get home and call Jim Cox to brag about the great fishing.

Unfortunately, I didn't manage to return as quickly as I had hoped. Somehow, two weeks slipped by. I called Jim and asked if he wanted to go, but he was not available. He suggested that I ask his brother-in-law, Tom. Tom and Jim's sister recently moved to Twin Falls from Connecticut, and he, Jim and I have fished together a number of times. Tom is a college professor and a brilliant man, and he loves to fly fish. He has a delightful sense of humor and is fun to be with, so I readily heeded Jim's suggestion. Tom accepted enthusiastically.

Tom and I launched the boat and headed up the reservoir. I was going to run down Whiskey Slough, but Tom told me that, because of my enthusiastic endorsement, he and Jim had fished both Whiskey Slough and Antelope Bay a week earlier, and the fish were no longer there. They had needed to go clear to Grey's Landing about five or six miles up the reservoir to find fish, but they had enjoyed good success. I by-passed Whiskey Slough, but as I approached Antelope Bay, I decided that since we were going right past it, we ought to at least stop and make a few casts. As I had done two weeks before, I drove to the far end and threw out the anchor.

Tom and I strung up our poles, and I made my first cast. I counted my fly down to the bottom and was making my retrieve when suddenly my line stopped. "Aw nuts," I thought, "I've snagged a rock." I gave my line a vigorous tug, and that rock took off like a rocket and sailed out of the water with a spectacular leap. I had hooked a real hog. It ripped my retrieved line off the bottom of the boat and leaped again. It tried running for deep water, but I managed to turn it. I worked it close to the boat, and it dived under the anchor rope. I worked it back and managed to pull it beneath the rope without getting tangled or snagging the dropper fly. I reached for it with the net, but it decided that it wasn't yet done, and it took off again. I set the net aside and settled down to enjoy another prolonged battle, but my line suddenly went slack. "Aw crap," I exclaimed! "He got off." I pulled in my line and found that my leader had broken near the butt, and I lost the fish and both of my flies.

We caught several more nice fish before things slacked off. There was a stiff wind blowing which was perfect to move the boat from where we were toward the open water of the reservoir. We decided to drift fish. We caught a fish or two and had at least a strike on each drift, but what activity we got was all in the shallow end.

"Ok, Tom," I said. "Show me where the fish are." I turned the boat, and we headed to Grey's Landing. By the time we got there, the wind had ceased blowing, and the algae, which had been wretched almost all summer, was beginning to clump on the surface. It should have been gone this late in the season, but the water was warmer than expected, and the alga was alive and well. We tried to fish, but after each cast our flies were coated with green slime, and it was hard to clean off. It was hopeless, and the whole upper end appeared covered with the thick gunk. I said, "I suggest we go back to Antelope Bay." We had not noticed any algae there. Tom readily agreed.

I sped back down the reservoir, swung into Antelope Bay and—AW CRAP! There was a boat parked right where we wanted to fish. The bay is narrow and there was no option to fish alongside it, so Tom and I headed on down the reservoir and turned into Whiskey Slough. There were two boats trolling at the mouth of the slough, but nobody at the far end. I ran down the slough, parked in 10 ft. of water, and Tom and I began catching large fish almost immediately. One of the boats that had been trolling, followed us down and parked about 60 ft. away on the deep side. They fished for a while and caught nothing, so they started their boat and idled slowly past us. Since the slough is narrow where we were, and we could almost cast to the bank on either side of my boat, they went right through the water we were fishing. That was aggravating enough, but then they parked about 60 ft. on the shallow side in about 7 ft. of water and began fishing with worms. They started catching fish immediately and tossing those big guys into their cooler. I figured they would probably catch their limits, there would be 12 less of those big trout in Whiskey Slough, and those guys would have far more fish than they could hope to eat. I was disgusted. Furthermore, since they passed us, the fish seemed to have moved from where Tom and I were fishing, and we could only sit there fuming and wishing we had gone about 60 feet farther down the slough.

By then the algae was so thick it was difficult to fish anyway, so we gave up and called it quits. We returned to the dock and a circus began. Jim Cox and I fish together frequently, and we've got launching my boat and taking it out of the water down to a fine art. When we return from fishing I let Jim off the boat at the dock. He backs the trailer into the water, and I drive the boat onto it and attach the winch. He pulls the boat out of the water and up the ramp. We both hop out and secure the boat to the trailer, and we are ready to roll. The whole operation takes just a few moments.

I had no idea how much experience Tom might have had backing a trailer, so I asked him if he wanted to give it a try. He said, "I think I can do that," so I handed him the truck key, and he climbed onto the dock and started for the truck. I backed the boat back away from the dock and waited for him to return with the trailer. Tom climbed into the truck, but, for some reason, instead of backing the trailer onto the boat ramp, he took off forward, drove in a big circle around other parked rigs and headed down the ramp nose first. He apparently was not used to having a trailer behind him because he cut his circle too sharp and clipped the tail light of a parked trailer breaking the lens. He drove down the ramp until he was close to the water, cut a big circle in the opposite direction and started back up the ramp. Had he backed the trailer onto the ramp from our parking spot, he would have had to back it only 60 or 70 ft., but by the time he now got the trailer straight he was 100 ft. up the ramp.

He began slowly backing toward the water. The trailer began to drift to the left. He over-corrected, and the trailer swung sharply to the right. He over-corrected again, and the trailer swung once again to the left. This time it was cramped too much to correct going in reverse, so he pulled the trailer forward. He started back down again, and the trailer went left, then right, then left, then right. Tom would stop periodically, pull up the ramp a ways and start again. His path down the ramp would have made a sidewinder proud.

A family was on the other dock launching their boat. They quit what they were doing to watch this show, and they were cracking up. Tom had the truck window down and could hear them laughing and making snide observations, and he was humiliated. Meanwhile, I was sitting out in the boat waiting—and waiting—and waiting. Finally, he got the trailer into the water, but it was askew, and he backed it just a little too far. I drove the boat onto the trailer by barely clearing the end corner of the dock. The front end of the boat made contact with the trailer, but the stern was still afloat. I stood up to go to the front of the boat and secure the winch. The guys on the next dock were talking loudly to each other, and Tom thought they yelled, "Pull forward" so he took off. "NO TOM, STOP!" I screamed. He did, but the guys on the dock were again roaring with laughter. I raced to the front of the boat, laid on my stomach, reached as far as I could, and just barely got my fingers onto the winch hook. I secured it to the boat and wound it tight against the trailer. "Now go," I called to Tom. He pulled the boat up the ramp a few feet, and the rest of the travel prep went smoothly. Tom left a note with his name and address on the truck windshield of the trailer with the broken tail light, and we started for home. Tom could see the humor of his trailer backing performance, and we had a good laugh. How often do we get an opportunity to so thoroughly entertain our fellow fishermen. I could laugh. I'm not a great trailer backer upper myself.

Tom and I were eager to get back out to Salmon Dam and try to get that spot in Whiskey Slough, so the following Thursday he, Jim and I were back on the water. The unseasonably warm weather had disappeared. The weather forecast had predicted wind 10-15 mph. but as usual they were wrong. It was more like 20 mph. with much stronger gusts. It was a little short of a howling gale, but the water was forming some pretty good whitecaps. As for the temperature, we wore winter coats all day.

We got our spot on Whiskey Slough because nobody else was dumb enough to be out on the water. I threw out the anchor, figuring it probably would not hold in that wind, but to my surprise, it did. We could not cast into the wind, so we could only fish off one side of the boat. If the wind caught our line just right, we could make some spectacular casts, but most of the time the wind blew our line down on our back-casts, and we were worried about hooking our buddies or slapping them on the back of the head with our fly. With three of us trying to fish, making decent casts was almost hopeless.

The wind was blowing right down the slough, so after I hooked Tom's hoodie and almost jerked his head off, we decided to try drift fishing. I pulled on the anchor rope and instantly realized why the anchor had held. It must have been hooked on a rock the size of the Titanic. I strained and tugged but to no avail. Jim grabbed the rope and the two of us heaved mightily—as mightily as two old septuagenarians can heave—but the anchor would not budge. I started the boat and headed into the wind. When the slack was out of the rope, I gave the boat some throttle. It dipped precariously on the side the anchor rope was tied to and began arcing around the anchor when suddenly it shot forward. The anchor had come loose.

We were feeling dejected as we ran up the slough, as we figured we'd probably made the trip for nothing. After about a hundred yards, I turned toward the cliffs and killed the motor. We couldn't cast very far into the wind, so we dropped our flies into the water and started stripping line off our reels. Suddenly, my line began ripping off my reel much faster than I was stripping. I had a fish—and then Jim hooked one. We caught several fish on that short drift. I fired up the motor and ran up the slough way farther than I did the first time. Jim said, "Man, you're really going for a long drift this time." We started our drift in 37 ft. of water. We did not expect to find fish in water that deep, but we started catching fish almost immediately. We caught one small fish that was 12 inches, but all the rest were 17 inches or bigger, and all were fat, heavy fish. Drifting as fast as we were, it was hard to keep the fish on our hooks, and we lost two or three for every one we landed. It was spectacular.

We were really hammering them, but an occasional fish got its revenge. I hooked one hog that was a real leaper. It ran toward the front of the boat and then toward the stern. On one of its leaps, we noticed that both Jim's and Tom's lines were tangled around mine. The longer that fish fought, the more tangled our lines got. I finally got it within reach of the net, but just as I made a reach it slipped the hook and was gone. Jim, Tom and I stood there in dismay looking at the bird's nest that fish had created. We did not get our lines in the water for the rest of the drift. We could almost hear that fish laughing. The fishing was incredible all day long, and when we left we agreed that it was probably the best day of trout fishing we had experienced on Salmon Dam.

The following morning (Friday), the wind had quit, and a beautiful day appeared to be in the making. I said, "Man, if the weather is like this on Monday, I'm heading back to Salmon Dam." Clea replied, in a teasing voice, "No, you don't want to go fishing on Monday." I said, "Of course I do. When would I ever not want to go fishing?" She said firmly, "Carl, you REALLY do not want to go fishing on Monday." I stewed over that for a moment, and then it struck me. Monday was our anniversary. I'm no Einstein, but I'm smart enough to know that she was right. I really did not want to go fishing on Monday.

At Salmon Dam reservoir, towering basalt cliffs meet the water. On a high ledge, a pair of golden eagles built a nest that they return to year after year. One summer, I saw a pair of fledges sitting on the ledge outside the nest, and I wondered how in the world they learn to fly. The ledge is half way down the cliff, and there is nothing at the bottom but water. The fledglings must enjoy considerably more success on their first attempt at flying than the poor robin fledges I see my Schnauzer mauling in my backyard. The same is true for the thousands of swallows whose mud nests decorate the cliffs and the pigeons that nest in the cracks and crevasses. Other wildlife is abundant in the canyon. The steep hillsides abutting the cliffs are wonderful habitat for chuckars. Deer come off the sagebrush desert to drink at the reservoir, and foxes and coyotes prowl the hillsides hunting chuckars, rabbits and mice.

Each autumn, usually in early to mid-November, I take my boat to the shop to be serviced and winterized. For reasons that elude me, the serviceman always takes the drain plug out of the back of the boat and lays it in the trough at the stern end. I guess he does it as part of a thorough clean-up to make sure there is no bilge, but he never puts it back. Usually my first act when I pick up my boat is to replace that plug.

Recently, we had a very mild winter, and the unusually warm weather extended into March. The ice was gone from the reservoirs, so in mid-March I decided to put my boat in the water and try some early spring fishing. I attached the trailer to the pick-up and towed the boat to Salmon Dam Reservoir. I removed the rear clamps that hold the boat to the trailer, tied the end of the bow rope to my truck and backed into the water. The boat did not float off the trailer. Puzzled, I pulled forward a little and then goosed the truck backwards and hit the brakes. Still the boat stuck to the trailer. Oops! I forgot to unsnap the winch at the front end of the boat. I pulled forward, unsnapped the winch, and the launch then went as expected. I tied the boat to the dock, drove the truck up the boat ramp, parked it off to one side and leisurely walked back to the dock. I stepped into the boat and started the motor. While it was warming a bit, I untied the bow rope from the dock and stowed it in its bin. I was in no hurry, so I was taking my time. I backed away from the dock, idled out past the no wake markers and shoved the throttle forward. The nose rose high into the air, and the motor roared. The boat seemed to be incapable of gaining speed, and it would not plane out. It was almost as if the rear end was still tied to the dock. I looked to the rear and noticed that water was almost coming over the stern end. OH CRAP! I FORGOT TO REPLACE THAT PLUG! I flipped the bilge pump switch, and water shot three feet out of the pump orifice.

I quickly reversed direction and headed back to the dock, where I secured the stern end using the anchor rope. Now, at least, the sucker wouldn't sink. I then opened the hatch cover over the gas tank and battery. It was nearly full of water, and my spare gallon can of gas and bottle of outboard oil were afloat. The bilge pump was doing a heroic job, but it was losing the battle. I looked in the trough at the rear of the boat and did not see the plug. That put me into near panic. The trough is shallow, and I feared the plug may have bounced out at some point when I was towing the boat. I had visions of myself wrestling that boat full of water onto the trailer.

To my great relief, I found it at one end underneath the bundle of cables going to the controls. I shucked my coat and rolled up my shirt sleeve. I lay on my belly, reached over the stern clear to the bottom of the boat and located the hole. With great trepidation, I took the plug in my hand and carefully, in that 40 degree water, probed for the hole a second time. I can't fix much of anything without letting screws or nuts slip from my fingers when I try to replace them, and that's when I'm warm. If I dropped that plug, it was gone forever. Fortunately, I slipped the plug into the hole and got the threads aligned before my fingers went numb. It then took 20 minutes for the bilge pump to empty all the water. I don't know why I bothered to roll up my sleeve. When I reached far enough to get to the plug hole, the sleeve roll was under water, so my shirt got soaked anyway. Between forgetting to unsnap the winch, forgetting to replace the bilge plug, and getting wet, it was definitely not one of my better days. To top it all off, the fishing was lousy.

Bright and early one morning, I hooked onto my boat trailer and headed to Roseworth Reservoir. I arrived at the boat ramp at the crack of dawn, and there was not another soul around. I worked the boat into the water, parked my truck and headed out for a morning of fishing. Several hours later, I returned to the ramp and walked to my truck. I was in for a nasty surprise. The window on the driver's side had been smashed out, and a large rock was lying nearby. The inside of the truck had been thoroughly rifled, glove box open, stuff strewn, but nothing seemed to be missing. The only thing of value that I had left in the truck was a small GPS unit, but it was still there. Apparently, the thief was hoping I was one of those fishermen who left his wallet, cash or credit cards in the truck while he was out on the water. He must have been terribly disappointed.

What was baffling to me was the fact that there was no one around, and I had seen no vehicles arrive or leave. The road to the ramp runs right along the bank of the lake, so a vehicle would have been hard to miss. The reservoir is just off a little used highway that runs from Rogerson to Jarbridge, Nevada. There is hardly any traffic except the occasional rancher or sportsmen coming to the lake to fish. I concluded that somebody must have slipped in and out since I really wasn't paying that much attention to the road.

I was ticked off, but even worse than the broken window were the numerous small glass crystals on the seat of the truck. I couldn't brush them off without cutting my fingers. I got most of them off using my windshield scraper, but I couldn't get them all, and I couldn't sit on the seat without risking a rump full of slivers. I finally put my fishing vest on the seat and sat on that. At home I vacuumed the glass with my shop vac., and thought I had it all cleaned up, but I found occasional glass crystals on the floor for several years as they shook down out of the door.

The fishing had been good, so I got the window replaced, and two days later I returned. This time, when I returned to the ramp, I left my boat tied to the dock and walked to the toilet before I retrieved my truck. As I looked over the crest of the small rise, I saw a beat-up old brown car with the cargo rack on top piled about as high as was feasible with camping gear. Beside the car, was a scruffy, small man with about a week's growth of dark brown beard and scraggly long hair topped with a filthy baseball cap. He had on a ragged, plaid shirt and filthy jeans. He was throwing a stick that his two dogs raced for, competing to see which could get it first and bring it back. "Aha," I thought, "I wonder if this guy was here two days ago." I walked to him and struck up a conversation, during the course of which, I learned that he had been camped at the reservoir for two weeks. I wondered why I had not seen him. I suspected that his lack of visibility might have been by design. He hinted broadly that a handout would be appreciated, but, considering my suspicions, I was not particularly overcome with generosity regarding him. I loaded my boat and left.

A couple of weeks later, I was fishing at Salmon Dam. As I was ready to leave the water, I looked west, toward the cliffs, and what did I see? There was the old brown car, the guy and his two dogs. I figured he had probably moved to see if he could find better pickings. The car was parked on a mild incline, and the bald right rear tire was flat. He was in the process of jacking up the car, but he had not put blocks behind the other wheels. As soon as he had the flat tire off of the car, he turned to accept a stick from one of the dogs which, he then threw. As he turned back, he gently bumped the car. It wasn't much of a nudge, but it was enough to cause the car to roll just a bit and fall off the jack. He let fly with a barrage of foul language that could have been heard clear across the lake. This incident had nothing to do with my smashed window except my very high suspicion that this was the guy who did it. I confess. I laughed my head off.

# BRUNEAU DUNES—A CHANGE OF PACE

Jim Cox and I had been fishing at Crane Falls, which is near the C. J. Strike Reservoir, all morning and had caught nothing but a few very small bass. At lunch time, we were commiserating with another fisherman about the poor fishing, and he mentioned that he had fished at Bruneau Dunes the previous day and had done very well. Since we had to drive past the Dunes on our way home, Jim and I decided to leave early and give it a try. About mid-afternoon, we launched our tubes on the small pond at Bruneau Dunes, and I began kicking slowly toward the weeds on the far side, casting and retrieving as I went. I was about half way across when my pole bent violently, and a good sized bass flew out of the water. It landed with a splash and began circling my tube, turning me as it went. Another flying leap! Another splash, and the fish headed deep. It was my first experience with a large mouth bass, and it made a lasting impression. Those babies are good fighters. It was slow to tire, but I finally brought it next to my tube, reached over the side and flipped the hook out of its mouth. "Hey, Jim," I called, "I think we made a good move." "You think?" he asked, as he set his hook on a bass of his own.

We continued to catch a few bass, but as afternoon gave way to evening the bluegills began to bite. Jim and I fished the weeds around the periphery of the shallow pond and caught fish after fish. Some of the bluegills were the size of dinner plates. They exceeded, by far, the heft and the strength of the 7 inch and smaller bluegills I had caught in other places. The fish we were catching were mostly 9-11 inches with an occasional one hitting the tape at 13 inches. These babies were fun to catch and even more fun to eat. Since that day, Jim and I have made a practice of returning to Bruneau Dunes several times each year during April, May and the early part of June.

Bruneau Dunes is a state park named for the large dunes of fine sand that are the size of small mountains. It is an extremely popular place in the spring before it gets too hot to be enjoyable. People climb the dunes just for the fun of it. Children slide down on plastic discs designed for snow. Older kids and adults ski or snowboard down. There are two seep ponds at Bruneau Dunes. Both are enhanced during the early spring by water pumped in from the Snake River for irrigation storage. Both ponds hold bass and bluegill, but the large pond is over-run with carp. Both ponds get fished, but the small pond is the most popular. Around the end of May, the pumped water is shut off, and, with irrigation draw down, the ponds recede to their natural state and become over-run with weeds. From mid-June on, they are almost unfishable. The small pond is mostly about 7-10 ft. deep with 12-13 ft. troughs and depressions when the pond is full. It is a trophy bass fishery, and bass may not be harvested unless greater than 20 inches. One can keep as many bluegills as he wants regardless of size.

In April, 2013, Jim Cox and I were returning from the Salmon Dam Reservoir, and we stopped at the small convenience store at Rogerson to buy soft drinks. I began hobbling toward the store. Jim gave me a bemused look and asked, somewhat incredulously, "Are you limping?" "Yeh," I replied, "my left great toe is killing me. When I got home, I pulled off my shoe and sock. My left great toe was massively swollen, fiery red and exquisitely tender to touch. It looked like gout I thought, but I didn't see how it could be. I don't drink alcohol, Clea and I go easy on beef, and we don't feast on rich foods. How the heck could I have gout? After a miserable night, I called my doctor. A few hours later I sat in his examining room with my shoe off. Dr. Ippolito walked in, looked at my foot and said, "Good grief, you have gout!" He treated me with a pain killer and Colchicine, which I was to take three times a day for three days.

The Colchicine worked fast, and a day later, the gouty flare-up was regressing nicely, so Clea and I drove to Utah, as previously planned, to visit our daughter and her family. That afternoon I began visiting the commode with ever increasing frequency. Diarrhea is a known and expected side effect of Colchicine, and I had expected things might loosen up a bit, but I never expected the ripping diarrhea that developed that evening. Aside from stomach cramps, I did not feel sick. That night I went to bed, and as I dropped off to sleep I felt a powerful squirt. I shot upright in bed hoping upon hope that it was just gas, but my worst fear was realized. I had shit the bed! Clea and I arose, and she helped me change the sheets and the mattress pad. I cleaned up and changed my underwear and pajamas. We placed a thick, folded bath towel under me and, with trepidation, I lay down again. Once again, as I dropped off to sleep, there was, again, an alarming squirt. This time I arose, removed the towel and cleaned up again. I was deeply distressed. Nobody wants to shit the bed under any circumstance and especially not at somebody else's house.

I was bone tired, but I did not dare go to sleep, so I dressed and spent the night alternately seated on the sofa reading and sitting on the pot. It was a long, miserable night. By morning, I was exhausted. My son-in-law made a run to Walgreens and bought a package of Depends. I decided I was not too proud to wear a diaper if it meant a few hours of sleep. I skipped the morning dose of Colchicine, diapered up and went to bed. I didn't need the diaper. The diarrhea stopped abruptly with the cessation of the cholchicine, but, man, that stuff really cleaned me out. I didn't visit the crapper for the next three days.

By the time we got back to Twin Falls, the gout had cleared up entirely, so we loaded our 5th wheel and went camping at Bruneau Dunes. It takes only a couple of hours to make the drive, so we arrived there about mid-morning. As soon as the trailer was set up, I grabbed my float tube and headed for the small pond. It was early in the day, but the bluegills were biting like crazy. I caught a jillion of them in two or three hours. I returned to camp, grabbed my filet board and went to work on those fish. They each yielded two large filets, and I ended up with a large plastic bag full of them.

Clea and I knew that I should not eat much red meat because of the gout, so we decided that we'd substitute fish. Those filets, rolled in flour and fried in butter, were absolutely delicious, so Clea and I gorged ourselves with them for three days. We returned home and almost immediately, I had a gout flare-up—this time in my right great toe. I went on-line to do a little research. I brought up a list of foods rich in purines (the amino acids that are converted to uric acid in the body and cause gout). As I knew, the list for "high in purine" included red meat, shell fish and salmon, but then it stated, "all fish are moderate high in purine." OH NO! Clea and I had stuffed ourselves with bluegills and now those little suckers were getting their revenge.

Jim and I continue to go to Bruneau Dunes in the spring and Clea and I continue to camp there a couple of times. I continue to catch bluegills, and, now that my gout is under control, I continue to eat them—but, as those words of wisdom dictate, all things in moderation.

# IT'S MAGIC, HONEY

Magic Reservoir is named because of its relationship to the Magic Valley. And why is Magic Valley so-named? The most reliable sources say it was named because of the almost magical transformation that occurred when the desert received irrigation water. Another story I heard was that the valley received its name when a mother was standing with her young daughter watching as irrigation water raced down the canal for the first time. The young girl said, "Mama, where did the water come from?" and the mother replied, "It's magic, honey." I don't know the reliability of that account, but I rather like it.

Jim Sorenson and I slipped my boat into the water at the West Magic ramp and headed up the reservoir. Large German browns were beginning to move toward the Big Wood River to spawn, and rainbows were following them to feast on the eggs. As we traveled northward, the reservoir began to narrow, and since it had been drawn down, it was mostly too shallow to move a boat through. We had to stick to the old river channel, which pretty much hugged the left shoreline. By following the channel, we were able to move up the reservoir to the confluence of the Big Wood River and Camas Creek. Where these streams met, the channel became wider and deeper forming a large pool about nine feet deep.

I moved to the lower end of a large mud flat just above the pool and threw out my anchor. Jim strung up his fly rod and made his first cast across the channel. He drew no response to that cast nor the second. He made his third cast and was into his retrieve, when he suddenly flung his arms into the air. Most people lift the tip of their rod when they set the hook on a fish, but Jim had Parkinson's Disease, and when he started a lift it didn't always stop precisely where he wished. He threw his arms into the air almost flinging his rod over his head, and his legs began to twitch and jerk. He brought his arms back down, but kept the tip of his rod high. The rod was bending and recoiling violently. The fish ripped off a few yards of line, and Jim began to haul it back. The fish had other ideas and took off again. The battle went back and forth for some time, but finally Jim got the fish into the net.

It was a 25 inch German brown. Jim was ecstatic. He had to pull out his pill case and gobble a pill to settle his dyskinesia down.

He and I had a fantastic day catching both browns and rainbows. A guy from Jerome, in a float tube, was the only other guy on the upper end of the lake. He was doing extremely well using pheasant tail nymphs.

We returned home in a state of euphoria, eager to return and try our luck again. Two days later, he, Jim Cox and I eased our way back up the river channel. I again parked near the mud flat and we started catching fish. It was only a short time, though, until it was apparent that the word had got out. Another boat came up the channel carrying two guys and their float tubes. They anchored their boat below us and climbed into their tubes. Other guys with tubes descended from the river, and it was not long until there were six float tubes moving back and forth across the pool and up and down the channel. It was no surprise that the fish skedaddled, and then none of us caught anything. We returned home aggravated and highly disappointed. Within a week the reservoir was drawn down, so it was no longer possible to move up the river channel, and that fishing tactic was done. I have never again managed to catch the reservoir at the right time and under the right conditions to repeat what we had that day.

Magic Reservoir is a large 14,000 acre[6] lake created by the Magic Dam. Toward the upper end, Camas Creek joins the Big Wood River and pours water into the reservoir. When the reservoir is full it splits at the upper end and extends well up the Big Wood and several miles up Camas Creek. The reservoir is narrow on the upper end, but widens dramatically before it reaches the mini-town called West Magic. The main fish of interest are German browns and rainbow trout, but there is also a robust population of yellow perch and a few small mouth bass. All can grow very large. The largest perch I have caught have been from Magic Reservoir, and the only place I have even seen larger ones was in Black Lake near Olympia, Washington. The reservoir is generally an excellent fishery, but during lean water years it gets drawn down to the point that there is an insufficient residual pool to maintain large numbers of fish, and the Department of Fish and Game opens it to salvage fishing. When this happens, it takes the fishery a while to recover though not as long as one might expect—probably due to fish which have migrated up the Wood River or up Camas Creek. The water from the reservoir feeds the Richfield Canal, a large canal which sustains the farms on the desert near Richfield Idaho. A few trout escape from the reservoir into the canal, and they rapidly grow large feeding on fresh water shrimp. These fish are exceptionally desirable to eat, so when the canal water is shut off, fishermen rush to the canal where they catch fish from pools fed by a trickle of water. At least they did in years past. Recently, improvements were made to the head gate eliminating that trickle, so there no longer is water in the canal year around.

I have seen fish exhibit what could be interpreted as exuberance, leaping and rippling the surface, but I always thought this activity was more than likely related to feeding. Magic Reservoir is the only place where I have seen a fish involved in an activity that almost certainly was play. Jim Cox and I were fishing Magic on the deep end near the dam. It was evening, and the water was very still. Near the shore, I saw a small stick floating on the surface, and it appeared to moving by itself. It would move slowly, then stop, or move rapidly, then stop. Over and over it happened. I was intrigued and baffled, and the stick held my rapt attention. After it had moved several times, I noticed that a fish was pushing it. The fish would turn suddenly, sometimes making a small splash or ripple on the mirror-like surface, race in a small circle, return to the stick and give it a shove then race away again. It did it over and over. It was not just nudging the stick. It would push it several inches and sometimes flip it with its nose. It was very like a dog playing with a stick on the lawn. It certainly appeared to be having fun. I wondered if there were insects or some other food attached to the stick, so I finally moved the boat close to the stick and picked it up. There did not seem to be anything on it. Do fish play? I think maybe they do.

The first and most important task when fishing is to find the fish. One afternoon, Jim Cox and I were in the process of doing just that. We were on the lower end of the reservoir working our way along a ridge where the shallow water dropped off quickly to deep water. Jim had caught a couple of nice fish, but we had not really got into fish in significant numbers. Suddenly, I saw the head of a dog moving through the water which I thought was rather amazing, since we were a long ways from shore. The dog approached the boat. I was fearful he might drown, so I reached over, grabbed his collar and helped him clamber aboard. He was a large, long haired retriever of some sort. All that hair was like a big mop, so I got my shirt soaked just helping him into the boat, and then he shook himself which finished the job. He then seemed to feel that he owed me a kiss or two, so he pushed himself against me as close as he could get and tried to lick my face. Now I was really wet. I had been comfortably warm previously, but there was a mild breeze blowing, and now that I was wet, I was cold.

We pondered what the heck to do with the dog. There were a few other boats on the water, so we began going from boat to boat trying to find the dog's owner. Finally, one of the boaters said he believed the dog belonged to a float tuber, who had arrived in a black pick-up that was parked on the shore. We drove all the way to the shore near the pick-up, and I now got my feet wet dragging the resisting dog through shallow water to the dry ground. I hopped back into the boat, and Jim began backing away. As soon as we moved away from the shore, the dog plunged right back into the water and started swimming across the lake. Darned pooch! I hauled him back into the boat once more, and we headed toward the only float tube we could see.

When we got close, the dog bailed out of the boat and swam to the tube. We explained what had happened. We expected some gratitude for rescuing the pooch, but instead the guy was really ticked off. He couldn't fish with the dog trying to climb on his tube, so now he had to haul the dog back to the truck, and he was a long ways out. I felt it served him right for bringing the dog along in the first place. Apparently he had no concerns that the dog would drown. Sometimes gratitude is hard to come by.

Jim Cox and I were fishing way up into Camas Creek one spring day when the Magic Reservoir was full. There was a western grebe swimming nearby. Suddenly, a golden eagle appeared over a nearby hill, and as it approached the water, the grebe made a plunging dive. I didn't time the dive, but that bird was under water for a long time. Finally, the eagle rose on the air currents and drifted some distance away. The grebe popped out of the water many yards downstream. It was only moments until the eagle gracefully circled and returned a few feet overhead. Down went the grebe. The eagle glided away and once again gained altitude some distance from the water. This time the grebe popped up fairly near to our boat. Again the eagle returned, and the grebe went down a third time. The eagle then left and did not return. I've fished amongst grebes many times and watched them do their dives for whatever it is they dive for, and I have marveled at how long they could hold their breath, but the length of time this lonely grebe stayed under water was truly remarkable.

# IN LOVE WITH MACKAY

On a beautiful day the middle of August, I steered my pick-up into the Joseph T. Fallini Campground and Clea and I gazed in awe at the beauty of the Mackay Reservoir and the well-groomed campground. Mt. McCaleb and the Lost River Mountain Range towered over the reservoir on the northeast side, and the Pioneer Range rose to the southwest. It was close to noon on a Monday, and the campground was almost empty. We found a pull-through trailer pad right on the water's edge, and I nabbed it. Clea loves to gaze through the trailer windows and watch the boats on the water, so the location was perfect. The lake was almost screaming, "Get out here and fish," so I quickly got the 5th wheel situated and headed for the boat ramp. The boat ramp was well situated on the lower third of the reservoir and had just the right slope to make for easy launching.

With great anticipation, I eased the boat away from the dock and turned toward the upper end of the reservoir. I was ripping along at full throttle when I began to see Smart Weed poking above the surface. The water was still 20 feet deep. Those had to be some very tall weeds. Shortly, the weeds became very dense. Seeing no way I could fish in that stuff, I turned back until I was below the weeds and headed for the far shore. There was a mild breeze blowing down the reservoir, so I decided to try drifting while casting toward the shore. The tactic worked well, and I was required to start the motor and make small corrections infrequently. The fishing, on the other hand, was terrible. I drifted all the way from the weeds to the dam, and I caught only six fish. There did not seem to be any fish at the dam, so, late in the afternoon, I returned to the trailer less than inspired by Mackay fishing.

The next morning I arose at dawn and once again ran up the reservoir to the Smart Weed. I had seen some guys fishing from the shore near the campground, so I decided to try drifting the near shore. I was just beginning my drift, when two guys launched a boat from the upper boat ramp which is about a mile above the campground. They hopped aboard and ripped across the lake to the far side. Just before reaching the shore, they turned into the Smart Weed without even slowing down and continued toward the upper end, where they disappeared amidst the willows. "If those guys can get through those weeds," I thought, "so can I."

I reeled in my line, set my rod on the floor, fired up my boat and zipped across the lake. I turned into the weeds with somewhat tenuous feelings, but to my astonishment and delight, after about 200 ft., I entered into a broad, weed free channel which immediately split. The left channel continued almost straight up the reservoir, whereas the right channel curved to the right, and after a few hundred feet it curved back to the left, then ran almost parallel to the left channel. The other boat had taken the left channel, so I decided to see how far up the right channel I could go. As the water got shallow, I slowed to an idle and slowly made my way. When my sonar indicated that I was in 7 ft. of water, I began to see fish rising—dozens of them.

I immediately lost my desire to explore and threw out my anchor near the weeds. The channel was about 50 to 60 ft. across, so I stood on the bow and began casting toward the weeds on the far side. I made my first cast and began my retrieve. I had made only two or three pulls on my line and wham! I had a fish. It was not very big, but it was feisty. It shot around the boat like a rocket, making multiple leaps. I got it alongside the boat and grabbed the leader with my hand, but I couldn't get the little beggar to stop flopping long enough for me to get a hold on the hook. Finally, I slipped the hook from its lip and made my second cast. wham! The same thing happened on the third and the fourth casts. The fish weren't just grabbing the fly, they were pounding it. I caught a fish nearly every cast all morning. It was incredible. A few of the fish were small but most were 14 or 15 inches with an occasional fish up to 20 inches.

Most of the fish were rainbow trout, but I also caught some cutthroats. A few brookies were in the mix, and I even caught a large mountain whitefish. On one cast, as I was pulling the fish toward the boat, I saw a flash of red which momentarily puzzled me, but when I got the fish close to the boat I found that I had hooked a male kokanee in full spawning colors. I was amazed. It was the first time I had caught a kokanee on a fly. I hadn't thought it was possible. After that first one, I caught several more and have since learned that catching them is a regular experience at Mackay.

Clea and I camped until the following Friday. I was on the water at dawn every morning and fished until about noon, enjoying that same phenomenal catch rate. Sometime between 11 AM and 1 PM a stiff breeze would come up, so I would beach the boat near our trailer and enjoyed other pursuits, not the least of which, was a long afternoon nap. If the wind subsided, I went back out on the lake in the evenings.

As a boy growing up in Downey, I occasionally heard one of the local farmers excitedly reporting a trip he had just made to the Mackay Reservoir, where he had caught some very large fish. Forty years later, when I moved my family to Twin Falls, I found that Mackay was just a two hour drive away. After I started fly fishing, I was eager to give the Mackay Reservoir a try, so I made a couple of trips with friends, and we fished from float tubes with very little success. Since there are many other reservoirs with good fishing near Twin Falls, I put Mackay out of my mind.

As Clea and I aged, we both developed sleep apnea and began using C-pap machines at night. That put an end to so-called dry camping, because we need electric hook-ups to run the machines. Camp grounds with hook-ups are scarce at reservoirs, so we were severely restricted as to where we could camp, and we became ever on the lookout for camp grounds with hook-ups. A few years ago, Jim Sorenson told me that he and his wife, while fishing the Big Wood River, had camped at the Mackay Reservoir. He reported that the campground was beautiful, reasonably priced and had full hook-ups for an R.V. My wife and I decided to give it a try.

The Mackay Reservoir is a 1392 acre impoundment holding 45,000 acre feet of water[7]. It fills the Big Lost River Valley above the Mackay Dam. The main source of water is the Big Lost River, but Warm Spring Creek, Parson's Creek, Farness Creek and Stockyard Creek all contribute. The creeks and the river all join together above the reservoir and then split into two large branches. The extent to which the creeks and/or the branches are obvious depends on how full the reservoir is. The Bureau of Land Management keeps the reservoir stocked with rainbow trout and kokanee, but wild cutthroat, brook trout and whitefish abound. There are also good numbers of wild rainbow, and I've caught occasional cutbows. From May through the summer months, catchable rainbows (9-10 inches) are dumped into the lake about every two weeks. These hatchery fish are triploids and therefore sterile. Kokanee stocking is less frequent, but large numbers of them run the river to spawn in the early fall. Most of the fishing is done from boats trolling the main body of the reservoir for rainbows or kokanee, but the fishermen who know the reservoir well get up into the weeds and willows which is where the big fish live.

The reservoir lies at the base of Mt. McCaleb in the Big Lost River Range. Mt. Borah, the highest mountain in Idaho, is just a few miles northwest. The campground at the reservoir was named Mackay for many years, but several years ago it was extended, refurbished and renamed the Joseph T. Fallini Campground. It is the only campground on a reservoir in the whole Challis Region that has full hook-ups.

After my incredible fishing experience, I could hardly wait to return to Mackay, so two weeks later on a Monday morning Clea and I found ourselves again pulling into the Fallini campground. We had been told by the campground host that the campground was usually only lightly inhabited on Mondays and tended to fill up during the week. Camp sites, on the weekends, were hard to come by. On this Monday, the camp site next to the water was again available. We liked the site because of the view for Clea and, for me, the fact that I could beach my boat just down the hill from the trailer.

We set up the camp and I got onto the water as quickly as I could and headed for the weeds. The water level had dropped considerably, and the two channels where I had fished before were no longer apparent. There were holes in the weeds, though, where I could fish. I did not catch fish every cast, but the fishing was still excellent. Around noon on my second day of fishing, I returned to our camp and beached the boat.

As I was dragging the bow of the boat up onto the rocky beach, I noticed a tall, lean man hustling down the steep hillside toward me. He hailed me and, with a pleasing Texas drawl, said that the camp host had suggested that he talk to me. His name was Tom Ridout and he and his wife, hailing from Ft. Worth, were touring the scenic parts of Idaho. They were traveling from Challis to Idaho Falls when they chanced upon the Mackay Reservoir, and the Fellini Campground looked like a good place to spend some time. Tom liked to fly fish, and he asked me where I thought he could do best from the shore as he had no boat or tube. I wasn't so sure he would have much success from the bank. He seemed like a likeable fellow, and I like company when I fish, so I told him he could go out with me, if he wished, and we made arrangements to meet at 6 AM.

The following morning, we shoved the boat off the rocky beach and headed for the weeds. Tom strung up his fly rod with a floating line. It was the only one he had. I gave him a Henry's Lake Renegade to tie on. I made my first cast and almost immediately hooked a fish. With hopeful anticipation, Tom made a beautiful cast—and came up with nothing. It was obvious from his casts that his experience was with a dry fly. He cast again and again and caught nothing. Meanwhile, I caught several fish. I put down my pole, and lifted my spare rod out of the storage bin. I strung it up with a 3 sink line and tied on a Renegade. I said, "Tom, try this." He put his rod down and took my spare. He made a lovely, arcing cast, and I told him to count the fly down about ten counts. He did so and began his retrieve. Wham! He had a nice 17 inch rainbow. The water was only seven or eight ft. deep, but it was necessary to get the fly near the bottom to catch fish. Tom continued to do well, and by noon he said he had never in his life caught so many fish nor so many large ones. He was absolutely delighted. I caught plenty of fish also, but, truthfully, I enjoyed watching Tom hook them more than catching them myself. It was a wonderful morning, and I was thankful to the fishing Gods for giving me a fine fishing day to offer Tom instead of locking the fish's mouths shut, as so often happens when you really want to do well.

Tom and his wife went on their way, and at the end of the week, Clea and I returned home. About two weeks later, I received a small package in the mail. Inside was a beautiful hand carved bowl. On the underside it was inscribed with Tom's name and the wood identified as Brisel Cone Pine. It is a work of art, and I keep it on my desk to hold address labels and notes. I treasure it highly. It is a constant reminder to me that small acts of friendship are repaid many times over.

The shore below our camp was moderately steep down to the water line. I referred to it as a beach, but there was no sand. The "beach" consisted of fist sized rocks. The first several trips we made to Mackay, I put my boat in the water at the boat ramp and then, when I was finished fishing, I dragged the bow up onto the beach below our trailer and tied it to a clump of willows. It was very convenient. One afternoon, the boat was beached and a howling gale arose from the west. It pushed my boat farther onto the beach and rocked it violently back and forth, pounded by the waves. The bottom was taking a real grinding from the rocks. I saw what was happening to my boat, but there was nothing I could do about it while the wind was blowing. When the gale subsided, I had a real struggle pushing my boat back into the water, and the rocks had thoroughly scrubbed the finish off a large portion of the bottom. The boat is aluminum, so there was no functional damage, but that was the last time I beached it. In recent years, we have not been able to acquire the water front camp site anyway, so I just put the boat in and take it out of the water as needed.

When we go camping, we take our little Schnauzer, Gracie, with us. I take her on the boat with me when I fish. When she is with me around the campground, I keep her on a leash, but often when I launch my boat there is nobody around the boat ramp, so I let her run while I get the boat into the water. She really enjoys being free to poke around a little bit. One evening I took her for a walk on the beach. I was a good distance from the trailer sites, and I decided to let Gracie go for a run.

Just as I reached down to unhook her leash, I saw some movement toward the water. I turned and was astonished to see a skunk not 20 ft. away from me. It was faced toward the water and was pre-occupied with something amidst the rocks. It had its nose down and was digging with one foot. Oh, man, I was glad I had not let Gracie loose. I turned and carefully walked away, towing a resisting Gracie, who seemed to think it would be marvelous to make the skunk's acquaintance. As far as I know, the skunk never even looked at us.

I have since wondered what we would do if Gracie got skunked. We'd bathe her, for sure, but a tomato juice bath is the suggested deodorizer, and we generally do not have tomato juice with us when we camp. We cannot leave her outside at night. How would we sleep with a skunked dog in the trailer? How would we endure her in the truck to ride home? I hope I never have to figure it all out.

One year, about mid-July, Clea and I were again camped at the Fellini Campground. It was an excellent water year, and the reservoir was showing hardly any draw down. I was doing my fishing way up the reservoir in the river and creek channels, amongst the willows. One of the channels entered the reservoir after running through a grassy meadow. With the water as high as it was, the meadow was flooded to a depth of four or five feet, and the channel was two or three feet deeper. At the far end of the meadow, there was a pole fence that crossed the channel and prevented a boat from proceeding farther upstream. I crossed the meadow and anchored near the fence. I caught a fish or at least had a strike nearly every cast. That channel was loaded with fish.

I pulled my cell phone from my pocket, called Jim Cox, and reported the excellent fishing. That evening he drove to the town of Mackay, which is six miles below the reservoir, and stayed in the Wagon Wheel Motel. We met at the boat dock at 6 A.M. and headed up the reservoir. Jim Cox is an excellent fisherman, and he invariably catches more fish than I do. That is difficult to do if one is catching fish nearly every cast, but somehow he manages it. We started on the meadow, and the fishing was hot. The meadow is small, though, and with two of us fishing, we eventually wore out our welcome. We began moving down the channel a few yards at a time, catching fish until they got wise and then moving again.

As we approached the junction where the channel we were fishing joined the Big Lost River Channel, we heard a peculiar pop, pop, pop noise almost like a miniature John Deere Tractor. In a moment or two a Sun Valley Fishing Guide appeared towing two clients. I had encountered him almost every day that I had fished the reservoir that summer. He rode on a small pontoon boat propelled by a tiny gas motor, and he towed his clients, in float tubes, behind him. He invariably went as far up the Big Lost as he could go, and then he and his clients waded the river and fished.

Jim and I fished where we were for a while and then Jim said, "Why don't we see how far up the river we can go?" We pulled up the anchor and made our way up the river channel. I tilted the motor to keep it off the bottom, and we worked our way around the curves. About the time we were far enough up the river to get beyond the reservoir back-up, we spotted the guide and his clients fishing the next curve up stream, so we tossed the anchor into a willow, and, as the boat swayed in the current, began to fish. As expected, the fishing was excellent, and we caught some very large trout. We followed the same routine we had used before—fish until the fish stopped biting, pull the anchor from the willows, float downstream a ways, pitch the anchor into another willow—it was fantastic. About a quarter of a mile downstream from where we started, we reached a large, sweeping bend, and the water was a little deeper. Brook trout were stacked in that bend like cord wood. I had two flies on and cast after cast I caught brookies on both flies. If they didn't grab the flies simultaneously, a fish would nab the second fly before I got the first fish to the boat. Some of them were really nice fish, but many were not very large, so it didn't take long to pull them to the boat and release them. I've never before or since caught so many fish in so short a period of time. Jim was doing the about same thing, but I was at the front of the boat and had a better casting angle. For an hour or two, I actually caught more fish than he did. I probably caught more fish that day than any other single day in all my years of fishing.

In the fall, after it got too late to camp, Jim and I started running to Mackay on over-night trips, and we stayed in the Wagon Wheel Motel. During the good water years, there was a place at the lower extent of the weeds and willows where the river water hit the far bank and turned sharply toward the middle of the reservoir. There was a deep hole in that bend (deep meaning six to eight feet), and it was usually full of fish. We would leave the motel early, grab a quick breakfast at Amy Lou's Café, and try to get onto the water and into that hole before other fishermen showed up. That late in the season, on week days, it was usually not a problem, and the fishing was invariably incredible. The kokanee that we saw running the river in late August and early September were now drifting back into the reservoir to die. They were already almost dead and had large white patches of mold on their heads and backs. They did not bite, but we could see them easily in the clear water.

Late in the fall of 2012, Jim and I ripped up the reservoir at full throttle, swung over to the upper edge of that hole and pitched out the anchor. We immediately started hooking fish and often had on two fish at once. We were hooting and hollering and just having a marvelous time. Suddenly, I heard a splash behind me and turned to see a large Labrador about 150 feet from us romping in water about a foot deep.

We were way up the reservoir. Where the hell did that dog come from? Then I spotted a portable duck blind that some poor schlepps had gone to the trouble to drag up the lake. We had sped right past it. It was a very good blind, obviously, but one thing was apparent—there would be no ducks landing within a half mile due to the efforts of two old fools acting like junior high kids. We suddenly became very quiet, as it was not lost on us as to who had the shot guns. I guess the guys in the blind were prepared for the likes of us, though, as they set aside their guns, picked up their fly rods and fished.

The years 2013 and 2014 were very poor water years, and mackay did not fill. One Monday in 2013, during the middle of July, Clea and I parked the trailer in the Fellini Campground. Since it was early in the season, I had left home with great visions of running up into the river, moving around amongst the willows, catching jillions of fish and, maybe, getting into those brookies again. I was shocked and disappointed to see that the upper edge of the water was already below the weeds and willows. The water was so low it was barely possible to launch my boat at the main boat ramp. I thought maybe I could get into the river channel and work my way into the large bend where Jim and I usually fish late in the fall, but after flailing around in water two feet deep and churning up mud with the prop, I gave it up and started trolling in seven to nine foot water.

I caught a lot of fish, but many of them were small. A few were 14 to 16 inches, but most were either 9 to 10 inch catchables or fingerlings. What a thrill catching 4 inch fish! Many of the fish I hooked were Kokanee which have a soft mouth. They would be on the hook for a few pulls, and then they were gone. Never-the-less, I caught rainbow, kokanee and a few brook trout so it was fun—a whole lot better than not fishing.

On Thursday, my last day of fishing, I once again began trolling. As I crossed the lake, I noticed that from one spot I could clearly see the mouth of the river emptying into the reservoir, and I decided to see if I could work my way into it. I tried to find the old river channel, but it is tortuous, so when I did find it, it was hard to stay in it. I worked my way up to where the water was two feet deep, and then I'd hit the channel, and the water was four feet. I'd follow the channel a bit, and then find myself in two feet of water again. I went as high as I dared and found myself within fifty feet of the river mouth. To my delight, I found the water temperature had dropped from 62 degrees to 50 degrees. I started casting into that shallow, cold water, and I found myself into lots of fish—big ones. I kept fishing until almost noon when a stiff wind came out of the west, and the shallow water turned muddy, ending my hooking of the hogs. Since I had used the channel as best I could to get where I was, it was with some unease that I pondered how I would fare getting out of that muddy, shallow water with the wind blowing. Fortunately, the wind was blowing toward the deep water, and I escaped without so much as scraping the bottom. I wondered why it took me until the last day of fishing to find my way to the river mouth. Sometimes I think maybe I'm not too bright.

There are two reservoirs I frequently fish where ospreys nest, Mackay and Daniels. At Mackay, the nest is in a dead Alder, near the meadow, at the upper end of the reservoir. In July, one will invariably see two fledges sitting on a branch near the nest awaiting the return of a parent with a meal. The delightful adults glide silently over the reservoir until they spot a fish, and then they fold their wings and dive straight down like rockets. They hit the water with considerable force, but at the last moment they turn their bodies, so that they hit talons first and, then, when fortunate, fly off with their prize. I've been fishing when an osprey hit the water within 50 feet of my boat. Even when they snag a fish, though, they are not assured of a meal.

I was fishing one day when an Osprey hit the water and emerged with a fish. It was not a really large fish, but it was a load for the bird. It beat its wings frantically, trying to gain altitude. It finally climbed to about 50 ft. and appeared to have its load under control when, suddenly, a seagull appeared, and began to pursue the osprey. Almost simultaneously, a large pelican rose off the reservoir and began chasing the seagull. It was comical watching the Osprey desperately flapping its wings, trying to gain speed, followed by the seagull, followed by the pelican. I assumed that the gull was going to harass the Osprey and try to make it drop the fish. The Pelican was hoping to nab the dropped prize before the gull had a chance to eat it. After a few moments they disappeared from my sight, so I concluded that the Osprey must have won the race, but it was just seconds later when the osprey returned and resumed hunting. The seagull returned also, no longer pursuing the osprey but still being followed by the pelican. I've wondered ever since which of the three birds, got to eat the fish. I'm relatively sure it was not the osprey.

Mackay also has a pair of bald eagles that nest on the west side of the reservoir. The nest is in a dead tree near the water's edge. The surprising thing to me is that it is not a very large tree, so the nest is not very high off the ground. Bald eagles do not dive into the water as the osprey do, but one day I saw one of them leave the tree, swoop low over the water, make a snatching grab with its talons and fly away with a good sized fish. These large birds are truly majestic.

# THE TREASURE OF MAGIC VALLEY

Jim Cox parked his Suburban on the road behind the westbound I 84 rest stop east of raft river, and we began the trek down the hill to the Snake River. It was early December and the steep face was covered with snow. I was wearing neoprene waders with heavy rubber boots attached, so I was not exactly tiptoeing through the tulips. I slipped and slid and barely averted falling on my fanny, but we finally arrived at the river's edge. "Step where I step and be careful," Jim admonished, "there are some really deep holes." The water was murky and moving swiftly, so it was difficult to see the bottom. Jim led the way, stepping from rock to rock, and I followed, trying to step almost exactly where he stepped, but he kept getting a little bit ahead of me, and he wasn't exactly leaving footprints in the water. I took one large step near the middle of the river that placed me on the edge of a rock shelf just an inch or so from a very deep hole. I looked down and saw how close I was to that edge and nearly froze to the spot. There was nothing to do but silently pray and keep moving. I wondered just what Jim was getting me into. I did not want him to think I was too chicken to do a little river wading, but getting across was dicey and it occurred to me that it wasn't going to be any better going back.

Once across we strung up our poles and began to fish. Jim waded out to a deep channel and almost immediately hooked a nice rainbow. I moved through shallow water several feet downstream from him to a chute of fast moving water with a deep hole at the bottom. I tossed my fly into the chute and watched it wash into the hole. Suddenly it stopped. "Aw, rats," I thought, "I've snagged a rock." I tugged on my line to pull it loose. It didn't come. I gave my line another tug and then noticed that it was moving sideways in the hole. I lifted the tip of my rod and began a steady pull, and a very large rainbow broke the surface and began running toward the current below the hole. I pulled it back so it couldn't get there and worked it toward the near side of the hole and up over the small ledge into shallower water. By now the fish was putting everything it had toward getting to the current, and I was holding fast and working it toward me. Suddenly, the hook snapped free and shot back toward me snagging in my coat sleeve.

"Well crap," I said, "I thought I had him. That was a nice fish." "You were horsing it pretty good," Jim laughed, "you should have let it run a little bit." "Yeh," I replied, "but I was afraid that if it got into that current it would get away." "It got away anyway," said Jim.

I've said before that I'm not a great stream fisherman. I lost that beauty and never touched another fish after all that wading. Jim caught several. The trip back across the river was not as bad as I had anticipated. Being familiar with where the holes were was hugely beneficial. The climb back up the hill that evening, though, was much worse than the trip down, and I did land on my backside a couple of times.

I consider the Snake River to be one of the treasures of the Magic Valley. If it were not for irrigation water from the Snake, the whole of Magic Valley would be a sage brush desert. And then there is the fishing. There are places where you fish it like a stream, and other places where it is more like still water. Sometimes it just depends on how high the water is. There are numerous reservoirs the whole length of the Snake and all are good fisheries.

When you drop a hook in any of the reservoirs or into the water in between, you never know what you are going to come up with. There are trout, small mouth bass, blue gill, crappie, perch, white fish, pikes minnows, suckers, chubs, cat fish, carp and sturgeon in there as well as some species I can't think of, and some I wouldn't know the name of anyway. I don't much care what I catch since I release them all. A trash fish isn't trash if it is on my hook. The important thing, to me, is to get the fish to take my fly.

One evening, I made the 15 minute drive from my house to Centennial Park in the Snake River Canyon. The boat ramp there is the best one I've ever launched from. People fish right off the dock, but I like to run my boat about a mile up the Snake to Pillar Falls. Small mouth bass fishing can be excellent when the bass are spawning. If the bass are not on the spawning beds, there is a big hole at the base of the falls, and one can fish in or around the hole. South of the hole, there is a large shallow area where schools of carp hang out. This evening I had driven my boat to the falls and stepped out onto a large, flat rock to fish. I was catching big suckers almost every cast.

Two guys in another boat came motoring up stream and pulled up next me, stepped out on the rock and walked a few feet away. They had large spinning rods, and they tied large sinkers onto their leaders and baited their hooks with pickled herring. They heaved those sinkers 50 or 60 feet and let them sink to the bottom. Within a short time, one of the guys jerked his pole upward, and, after a prolonged battle, lifted the head of a six foot sturgeon onto the shore. He quickly removed the hook and pushed it back into the water. He caught nine of them that evening in just two or three hours. Most of them were only three feet long, but still, those were impressive fish. I've never fished for sturgeon, but after that evening I was sorely tempted. I'd have to buy a lot of gear, though, so I elected to stick to fly fishing. I've caught trout, bass, pikes minnows (squaw fish) and suckers out of that hole, and I've wasted a lot of time trying, unsuccessfully, to entice those carp.

Jim Cox and Robert Norman both like to fish just below the American Falls Dam in the fall when the water is shut off to recharge the reservoir. I have fished there in the past, but it involves some fairly treacherous wading, and I, with bilateral total knee replacements, no longer care to risk slipping into one of the deep holes or falling on my butt. Those holes yield some truly spectacular fish. It is suspected by some that they obtain their huge size, in part, but feasting on their brethren who were unfortunate enough to get chopped up by the turbines.

There are numerous springs all along the Snake River Canyon, and the water temperature in the springs is usually around 50 degrees. One can sometimes fish directly in the springs or, if not, fish the Snake where the spring water runs in. One pleasant winter day, I was fishing the Crystal Spring near the Niagara Springs Park. I could see huge rainbow swimming around in the spring, and they were driving me nuts because I couldn't get them to bite. I suppose they could see me as well as I could see them. The spring isn't named Crystal for nothing. I had caught a couple of small trout and was about to give up fishing when I saw a Fish and Game guy walking toward me. I thought he was a warden. He smiled and said, "How is the fishing?" "Pretty slow," I replied. He chuckled and said, "It's about to get a whole lot better." I followed his gaze up the road and coming down the grade was a large tanker truck. It drove past and turned around then came back and stopped about 50 ft. from me. The driver hopped out of the truck, attached a large hose to the tank, and began pumping fish into the spring. I thought it would surely take a couple of days for the fish to get over the shock of the transport and start to bite but, to my delight, they came off that truck ready to chow down. I started catching them every cast. The guy was right—the fishing got much better. I'd still like to hook one of those big ones though.

# URBAN FISHING

The sun was sinking toward the horizon, and the water was flat as glass as I approached the dock in my float tube. I had fished the upper end of Dierke Lake earlier and had caught a few trout and a nice 17 inch largemouth bass. As evening approached, I moved down the lake and was kicking my tube in a large circle. From the dock, I kicked toward a buoy in the middle of the lake which serves absolutely no purpose that I have been able to discern, but it is a good landmark. From the buoy, I kicked at an angle up the lake and toward the reeds near the shore. I then turned and headed back to the dock. On this evening, the dock was lined from one end to the other with people fishing. A child about eight years old was standing, holding a small spinning rod. He set the rod down on the dock and walked toward his father. He had taken only two or three steps when his rod suddenly clattered across the dock and flew off into the water. The boy turned and ran back to where his rod most recently had been and stood staring into the water with a shocked look on his face. That rod was gone. I suspected it would one day become the property of a scuba diving student. The father was angrily berating the kid, but I had to laugh. The whole dock was lined with people, and the fish grabs the bait of the only untended pole. How did it know?

Dierke Lake is a seep lake about two thirds of the way down the Snake River Canyon just off the Shoshone Falls road. On the south side, there is a large city park and a swimming area separated from the main body of the lake by a well kempt dock. Dierke is the end lake in a chain of four or five lakes extending up the canyon. All the lakes but Dierke are called hidden lakes, because they can't be seen from Dierke itself. I have climbed the canyon wall and viewed them in the past, and I thought they were all just large puddles, but apparently one of them is very deep. Dierke is the only lake that has fish. It has been home to largemouth bass, blue gill and catfish for many years. During the summer, Fish and Game dumps a few hundred trout of varying sizes into the lake from time to time, and most of them are rapidly caught. The blue gill were so over populated that none grew larger than a half dollar until recent years when the Mosquito Control

District started netting large numbers of them and transferring them to silt ponds for mosquito control. Within a couple of years of netting them out, fishermen started catching blue gill up to nine inches. The transformation, with a little population reduction, was quite dramatic.

A couple of years ago, Jim Cox and I were fishing from the bank, and, to his astonishment, Jim hooked a crappie. We have no idea where crappie came from, but there is now a good population of decent sized ones in the lake. Dierke is a fun place to fish. If you can hit it shortly after a plant you can do very well catching trout from the shore, and since the plant usually includes several spawners and large albino (golden) trout, you stand a good chance of hooking a "big un." If you use a float tube in the evenings, you are almost sure to catch crappie, blue gill and maybe a few bass and trout. Fishing off the dock used to be good, but two or three years ago the powers that be made it illegal. This makes sense when the swimming area is open, but why all the time? I suspect it is because there are so many impolite and inconsiderate souls that persist in leaving smears of power bait, crushed salmon eggs, worms, gobs of mud, plastic bags, plastic containers, and beer cans on the dock just like they do on the banks of Dierke, and all around every other lake where people are permitted to fish.

No gasoline motors are allowed on Dierke, so one afternoon Jim Cox and I had one of our less than inspired ideas. We attached a small electric trolling motor to the rear of his 12 ft. boat and launched it into the lake. I have no thought as to why that seemed like a good idea, since the lake can be easily covered with a float tube, and one can put in a tube with little effort whereas the boat was a struggle. We forgot to bring along his regular 12 volt battery. We thought about going back to his house after it, but Jim had a small lawn mower battery in his Suburban, so he hooked it up to the trolling motor to see if it would work. The motor ran fine. Fish and Game dumps fish into the lake at the same place one puts a boat in. They had just made a recent plant, so we maneuvered across the channel, dropped the anchor, and caught quite a few trout just out from the launch area. We could have done as well from the shore, but what the heck, we had the boat in the water.

When we got tired of the easy pickings, we set out trolling across the lake. At Dierke there are extensive areas where shallow water

192

extends well out into the lake, and there is dense growth of reeds. You can't fish from the shore in those places. Our plan was to troll to the far end of the lake, park next to the reeds and see if we couldn't scare up some decent bass.

We had barely arrived at the far end when a strong gale suddenly developed out of the west. After we slapped ourselves on the back of our heads with our flies a time or two, we concluded that the wind was too strong for us to cast, and we couldn't get the anchor to hold, so we figured that maybe we'd better head back. Jim turned the trolling motor on high, but it was no match for the wind which kept pushing the bow around. I grabbed an oar and tried using it like a paddle to keep the boat straight, but we were going nowhere. We then discovered why we should have gone after the big battery when, after just moments, the little one ran out of juice. Jim grabbed the other oar and began paddling from the back of the boat. We still couldn't keep the boat headed straight. If I paddled on the opposite side from him the boat swung one way. If I paddled on the same side it turned the other way. We were going nowhere.

We finally worked the boat over to one side of the lake and tried to pull ourselves along using the reeds. We tore up a lot of reeds, and we did manage to make a little headway, but the wind kept pushing us into the reeds so we couldn't go, and we'd have to work our way back out. Then we would hit a gap where there were no reeds, and it was back to trying to paddle. The whole situation was totally ridiculous, and, at first, we were laughing so hard it nearly sapped our strength. By the time we were half way back our arms ached until we could hardly use them, and we'd have to stop, hold on to the reeds and rest. Somehow, the humor of the situation dissipated. Considerably later and after much sweat and strain, we finally made it as far as the dock. Jim climbed onto the dock, grabbed the rope and towed us to the far end. He got back into the boat, and we continued to fight our way along the reeds down the channel to the launch area. Again, after much sweat and strain we pulled into the passage leading to the ramp, breathed a sigh of relief—and the wind stopped as suddenly as it had started. Aw, crap! It was now dead calm, but we felt absolutely no inclination to go back out onto the lake, and we haven't put a boat in Deirke since.

In recent years, Fish and Game has become increasingly enthusiastic about so-called urban fishing. They can sprinkle a few fish in a small lake, like Dierke, close to town and keep a lot of people happy that probably would not venture out to the larger reservoirs. They seem to feel it is good utilization of their resources. These are put and take fisheries. Fish and game puts a few fish in and happy citizens take 'em out.

Another put and take fishery is the Filer Ponds. These were created a few years ago when the property owner allowed fish and game to stock his silt ponds with the stipulation that one pond would be kept for children only. The ponds are muddy due to silt, and the kiddy pond is moss filled in the summer time, but the ponds are spring fed as well as from irrigation run-off, so in the winter time the water becomes clear, and the trout fishing, at times, excellent. Again, it is good to keep track of the Fish and Game stocking schedule.

The ponds are only 10 minutes away from my house, so they are a good place to go on a nice winter day when one has fishing fever and only a few hours to kill. I took my eleven year old grandson there to catch his first fish. I had taken him out onto the front lawn and showed him how to cast a fly, and then we headed out to the kiddy pond. It was heavily stocked with fish including some large spawners. On his first cast, he hooked a big guy that about dragged him into the water. It got off before he landed it, but he caught several more, two of which he dutifully hauled home and demanded that his mother cook them. She did, and he declared the fish delicious, but, strangely, he since declines when offered a meal of fish.

# THE IMPORTANCE OF FISHING

I grew up in a very funny family. Our gatherings were a riot of laughter and fun. The funniest of all of us was my brother, Lyle. He was ten years older than me and was the smartest man I ever knew. He became an Internist/Cardiologist. When he was in residency training, he once told me that his idea of a pleasant evening was to sit down and read a stack of medical journals. That sounded like an absolute drudge to me, but then to each his own. Medical journals aside, Lyle knew how to have a good time. Since he was so much fun to be with, he was good at conning people into doing work for him. One time he was painting his house, and he persuaded Jack, my eldest sister's husband, and Una, my youngest sister to help him. He assigned them the task of plastering and texturing a ceiling while he painted an adjacent room. As the evening wore on, he returned to the room and burst into laughter. Una was filling a toilet plunger with plaster and applying it to the ceiling. Jack was on a ladder with a trowel smoothing and texturing the mud as soon as it was applied. As unconventional as the operation was, it worked amazingly well. "How in the world," Lyle asked, "did it ever occur to you to use a toilet plunger?" Una replied, "Well, you gave us the shitty job—ergo toilet plunger."

Lyle loved to fish. In fact, I'm quite sure he liked it more than reading journals. He was a bait fisherman, though, and I don't think he ever tried fly fishing. I regret that I never had a chance to fish with him as we lived a considerable distance apart, and he died at age 50. I cite the following story as an example of the priority of fishing in our lives: Lyle wanted a new car, so, as soon as he could afford one, he bought a new Buick. He had always wanted one, so he was sorely disappointed when it turned out to be a total lemon. He would start the car in the morning and head for the hospital. On frequent occasions he would get only a few blocks, and the car would stall and smoke would pour out from under the hood. It would not restart. On each occassion he had to call a tow truck and have the car towed to the dealership. By the time the car was in the garage, it would start and run perfectly. The mechanics could never find anything wrong with it. After the third time, Lyle began to sense that the mechanics thought he was a crackpot He did not know what was worse—the fact that the car malfunctioned or the disdain of the mechanics. One afternoon, as Lyle was driving along, there was a loud WHOOSH, and a ball of orange flame and black smoke shot out through the grill. Lyle jumped out of the car, ran to the trunk and opened it. Then, by his account, he first grabbed his fishing pole, then his tackle box and then his black medical bag—in that order. He then ran back up the street to a store with a pay phone (there were no cell phones in those days). By then his car was completely engulfed in flames, and thick, acrid black smoke was rolling skyward. He called the fire department and then the Buick Dealer to whom he calmly reported, "You know that car of mine? It's smoking again."

# FLY ROD MISHAPS

I've always considered that I take loving care of my fly rods, but my history would suggest otherwise. My fly fishing friends had advised me that, with a fly rod, it was not a question of if you would break it but rather when. Accordingly, I spent a little more (actually quite a bit more) and acquired rods with a life time guarantee. There are a number of excellent rods on the market, but I bought Sage rods. I regard Sage as an excellent company. I'd have to say, I've got my money's worth.

The first rod disaster I witnessed was not my own. Jim Cox, Bob Norman and I were fishing the Treasureton Reservoir near Preston, Idaho. We were in Jim's boat, so he was sitting at the rear managing the motor. We had been fishing for a while without catching any fish, so we decided to change locations. We all reeled in our lines. Bob and I were holding our flies out of the water, ready to move. Jim set his pole on the bottom of the boat since he needed one hand to steer the boat and the other hand to work the shift lever. He did not notice that his fly had dropped into the water behind the boat. He dropped the shift lever into reverse and began backing the boat away from the dam. Suddenly, the reel end of his rod shot into the air and began pumping violently up and down. The propeller had caught his leader and then the tip of his rod. Jim grabbed for the shift lever, shoved it out of gear and began unwinding his rod. Something akin to a strangled sob escaped him as he held the rod before him with the tip end resembling a broken spring. Robert and I were beside ourselves laughing. Fortunately, Jim had a spare rod, so we continued fishing.

The first time I broke a rod, I was fishing with my son-in-law at Henry's Lake. We had been out in float tubes all morning and decided to take a break for lunch. We tossed the tubes into the back of the pick-up. Since we were going to return for the afternoon, I did not unstring my rod. I pulled it apart, folded it double and shoved it into my rod case, leaving the handle and reel sticking out of the zippered end. I did not realize that I had put some tension on the line when I pushed the rod into the case. Just as I slammed the pick-up door, the tip end of the rod came flying out of the case like an arrow shot from a bow. It made it about half way out the door at which point it was completely crushed.

My second mishap occurred when I was fishing Salmon Dam. I was finished for the day and had just pulled the boat out of the water. At that time, I had a small boat I carried on top of my pick-up. I lifted my fly rod out of the boat, pulled it apart and set the two halves into the bed of the pick-up while I winched the boat onto my boat rack and secured it. I then picked up the anchor from the ground and tossed it into the bed of the pick-up. Just as it left my hand I remembered the rod, but it was too late. I snatched the rod from under the anchor, but the tip end dangled over my hand like a wilted daisy. Swearing didn't help at all.

I bought an inexpensive 5 wt. rod to use when fishing Rock Creek. I had finished a day of fishing and was making the steep climb out of the canyon. I was wearing felt soled wading boots over my waders. The felt soles were excellent when used for their intended purpose, which was to keep one from slipping when wading in water. The wet felt on canyon wall rocks was another story. I was half way out of the canyon when my feet shot out from under me, and I went down hard—right onto my fly rod. The rod actually survived, but the reel didn't fare so well. I lit on it with my right hip which bent the spool and snapped the small bolt holding the handle. I thought it was a total loss. As it turned out, I fared worse than the reel. My hip was sore and bruised for two weeks. I managed to straighten the bent spool, and I found a small bolt that fit the handle. I fixed the reel and it still works.

I wrote in the chapter on Roseworth about losing a rod into the lake. On that occasion, my life time warranty did me absolutely no good

The last rod I destroyed was at Filer Pond. I treasure it as a place I can quickly get to and kill a couple of hours when we get the occasional warm, windless winter day. On one of my trips to the pond, I had been fishing for a while and, being an old gomer, I had to pee. I walked to the outhouse next to the parking lot, propped my rod against the front wall and went inside. The door was spring loaded assuring that it would stay shut when the facility was not in use. When I had concluded my business, I exited, as one would expect. Just as I let go of the door, a gust of wind caught my pole causing it to fall toward the door. I made a grab, but the door spring was strong, and I was too slow. The door sheared away six inches of the tip end. It was, of course, my best rod. I wondered how long the boys at Sage laughed over that mishap: FISHERMAN LOSES ROD TO CRAPPER DOOR! Since that rod model was no longer in production, Sage built me a complete new rod. On the two previous occasions when I broke rods they just replaced the broken tips. As I said earlier, Sage is a great company.

There is absolute joy to fishing, and it extends well beyond the catching of fish. That, of course, is the main event, but I've been on the water many times when I didn't touch a fish, and I came home feeling exhilarated. There are other fishermen to talk to and sometimes they do funny things. There are also any number of wild creatures to observe, and they can be most entertaining. It is a rare day on the water when one does not observe something amusing or truly wondrous from the creatures God put on this earth

# ACKNOWLEDGMENTS

It is unlikely that this book would have happened were it not for the persuasion of my good friend, Delene Covert, who encouraged me to save my stories. I am hugely indebted to her, also, for instruction regarding punctuation which, I have learned, is not my strong suite. I also owe a debt of gratitude to my many fishing friends, especially Jim Cox who taught me to fly fish, his brother-in-law, Tom Schultz, Robert Norman who is the best fisherman I know and Jim Sorenson. All are featured prominently in the book.

# BIBLIOGRAPHY


Wikipedia
Wikipedia
Wikipedia
Visit Idaho website
Wikipedia
Visit Idaho website
Wikipedia

CPSIA information can be obtained at www.ICGtesting.com
Printed in the USA
LVOW07s0038240915

455514LV00001B/139/P